Penguin Critical Studies
Advisory Editor: Bryan Loughrey

The Poetry of William Blake

Michael Ferber

Penguin Books

PENGUIN BOOKS

Published by the Penguin Group
Penguin Books Ltd, 27 Wrights Lane, London W8 5TZ, England
Penguin Books USA Inc., 375 Hudson Street, New York, New York 10014, USA
Penguin Books Australia Ltd, Ringwood, Victoria, Australia
Penguin Books Canada Ltd, 10 Alcorn Avenue, Toronto, Ontario, Canada M4V 3B2
Penguin Books (NZ) Ltd, 182–190 Wairau Road, Auckland 10, New Zealand

Penguin Books Ltd, Registered Offices: Harmondsworth, Middlesex, England

First published 1991
10 9 8 7 6 5 4 3

Printed in England by Clays Ltd, St Ives plc
Filmset in Monophoto 9/11pt Times

Penguin Critical Studies

PEN MARKS NOTED 11/21OO.   T

**This book is to be returned on or before
the last date stamped below.**

RENEWALS   Please quote: date of return, your ticket number
and computer label number for each item.

Penguin Critical Studies

The Poetry of William Blake

Michael Ferber is a Professor of English at the University of New Hampshire. He holds a Ph.D. in English from Harvard and has taught at Yale. From 1984 to 1987 he worked for nuclear disarmament at the Coalition for a New Foreign Policy in Washington. His book The Social Vision of William Blake was published in 1985. He is also the author of The Poetry of Shelley in the Penguin Critical Studies series.

Contents

Preface

This book discusses in detail most of the poetry and prose Blake wrote during a brief but wonderfully creative period, from 1789 to 1794: *Songs of Innocence*, *Songs of Experience*, *The Book of Thel*, *Visions of the Daughters of Albion*, *America: A Prophecy* and *The Marriage of Heaven and Hell*. The final chapter looks ahead to his later and longer poetry.

All of these works were composites of writing and picture, or 'illuminated' texts. Some of the designs are discussed here, and their bearings on the meaning of the texts is considered, but mainly as examples of how to approach the works. The emphasis is on the words.

Except for the first chapter, this books presumes that its reader has already read the Blake books and, like Blake's original readers, has some familiarity with the Bible and Milton's *Paradise Lost*.

All poetry quotations are from Alicia Ostriker (ed.), *William Blake: The Complete Poems* (Penguin, 1977), and prose quotations are from David V. Erdman (ed.), *The Complete Poetry and Prose of William Blake* (rev. edn, Anchor Press, 1982). References to the Erdman text are indicated 'E', followed by the page number. All biblical references are to the King James Bible.

I would like to thank Susan Arnold, Sherrie Gradin, Rachel Price, Lauren Gail Smith and Jack Richardson for comments on early drafts.

Introduction

If Blake were brought back to life today, he would be astonished at how widely known he has become. A four-quatrain poem without a title, with which he introduced a long poem that has survived in only four engraved copies (*Milton*), is now the second national anthem of England under the title 'Jerusalem'. It concludes:

> I will not cease from Mental Fight,
> Nor shall my Sword sleep in my hand:
> Till we have built Jerusalem,
> In Englands green & pleasant Land.

A phrase earlier in the poem provides the title for the film *Chariots of Fire*, which concludes with church-goers singing the hymn.

If you walk along the south bank of the Thames, on the 'Silver Jubilee Walkway' near Westminster Bridge, you will come across another four-quatrain poem entitled 'London' chiselled into the stones at your feet.

> How the Chimney-sweepers cry
> Every blackning Church appalls,
> And the hapless Soldiers sigh,
> Runs in blood down Palace walls[.]

Another phrase from this poem, 'mind-forg'd manacles', has become absorbed in our speech as thoroughly as many lines from Shakespeare. All-night poetry marathons are now common on Blake's birthday. Since the 1960s, if not earlier, Blake quotations have appeared on walls and protest signs throughout the English-speaking world.

> A Robin Red breast in a Cage
> Puts all Heaven in a Rage.

Prisons are built with the stones of Law, Brothels with bricks of Religion.

Prudence is a rich ugly old maid courted by Incapacity.

The tygers of wrath are wiser than the horses of instruction.

(I carried a sign bearing this last one myself while a teaching assistant on strike at Harvard.) There are Blake ballets, Blake plays, even a Blake summer camp (called Golgonooza) in America. CBC Radio Canada broadcast a three-part Blake programme in 1987. Colourful posters of a bearded old man creating the universe, or of a nude young man dancing on a mountain top, adorn the walls of countless university students. In 1957 a postage stamp to celebrate the bicentenary of Blake's birth was issued by Romania (but not by the United Kingdom).

And yet to many of his most devoted admirers Blake still seems a private possession. They are often amazed to meet each other. So intimately does Blake seem to 'speak to one's condition', as the Quakers say, so thoroughly does he seem to move in and rearrange the furniture of one's soul, that to share him, to see him through the eyes of another Blakean, feels almost as threatening as to share one's wife or husband. This feeling, however, has not kept dozens of Blakeans from going public with 'their' Blake, very often grafted to other enthusiasms, with the result that we find on the library shelves a mystical Blake, a neo-platonic Blake, a gnostic Blake and a cabbalistic Blake, not to mention a materialist Blake who disliked mysticism, neo-platonism, gnosticism and cabbalism; a radical Blake and a conservative Blake; a heretical inner-light Protestant and an orthodox Anglican; a Jungian and a Freudian Blake; a spokesman of patriarchal oppression and a herald of women's liberation; a retrograde mythologist of origins and a precursor of the post-structuralist dissolution of all starting points. I myself am not exempt from having appropriated him to my purposes, as indeed no one is, but Blake has lent himself peculiarly to a sort of squeezing and stretching and assimilating that he himself, if he came back from the dead, would probably admit was inevitable. For he was the most private of poets (though less private as a painter and engraver), hardly known as a poet at all in his day, developing the most idiosyncratic of symbolic systems, while at the same time imagining himself, like Milton, a preacher and prophet to the nation, addressing his unknown works 'To the Public' or 'To the Christians', and dreaming up projects for great murals all over London. He also spoke on many registers, from the childlike and almost unbearably namby-pamby in some of his *Songs of Innocence*, through grim indignation and prophetic wrath, cheerful mockery and oracular incantation in his *Songs of Experience* and early 'prophecies', to the helpless lamentations and joyful recoveries in his late epics. His many voices have spoken differently to many different conditions but nearly always with the sort of intensity that reflects Blake's grasp of something continuous and common in these conditions, some way in which the 'Minute

Particular' that is each unique human being unites in essential empathy with all the brothers and sisters of our human family.

Blake is known to be a difficult poet. In his own day he was widely believed to be 'quite mad', though those who knew him best thought otherwise. Except for the *Songs of Innocence and of Experience*, then as now the most widely known and most admired of his works, his poetry was dismissed, deprecated, or, if treated respectfully, put in a special category almost beyond discussion and labelled as 'mystical in a very high degree' (William Thompson) or as a 'mysterious and incomprehensible rhapsody' (Henry Crabb Robinson). But even the *Songs* sometimes inspired such comments. Coleridge, after carefully reading and annotating them, wrote to the friend who had lent him a copy that Blake was 'a mystic *emphatically*', and an 'apo- or rather anacalyptic Poet, and Painter!' By revising his adjective from 'apocalyptic' (that is, 'revelatory', with a reference to the Apocalypse of St John), Coleridge may have intended the opposite meaning ('veiled', 'mysterious'), but 'anacalyptic' has an almost technical sense, owing to St Paul, of revealed or unveiled *sight* when we read Scripture in the light of Christ. If he meant it in that sense Coleridge had a fine insight into Blake, whose poems often seem to be visionary re-readings of Scripture, but Coleridge's friend could not have found it encouraging unless he himself felt divinely endowed with vision.

Today few of us take Blake's madness seriously, either because we don't believe in it or because it no longer matters. What was really 'sane', after all, about English society in 1810? 'Madness' is a social category as well as a medical one, and to use it as a label is to label oneself. 'Difficulty' would seem to be the same sort of category, for what appears obscure to one group may seem lucid to another. An army of Blake scholars has been hard at work for decades producing Blake dictionaries, concordances, annotated editions and systematic interpretations to make Blake more accessible to others. Many of the most influential scholars, moreover, have caught something of Blake's own confident, prophetic tone ('Mark well my words!' he tells us in *Milton*, 'they are of your eternal salvation!'), which may encourage beginners by showing them that at least *someone* understands Blake, but which is more likely to intimidate them when they don't find it as easy as that scholar seems to, or to give them the illusion of understanding when they master a few definitions and strange names.

This book assumes that Blake is difficult and remains difficult, but not so difficult that a beginner cannot reach the essentials, and take great pleasure in reaching them, without first climbing ladders of scholarship. Indeed some of the *Songs* are so simple, so much like the nursery rhymes they imitate, that the reader may wonder what subtleties he or she has missed. Many readers, on the other hand, will have grown up with 'Tyger, Tyger' and loved it precisely for the not-quite-reachable mystery at its heart. Sometimes Blake's meaning is blazingly obvious, yet it is so startling or threatening (the notion that you must die for your enemy, for example) that out of resistance to it the reader may go back over it in search of ironies or subtexts that subvert the plain sense, sooner wallowing in a slough of comfortable difficulties than going forth to meet the simple, disturbing assertion.

Then, too, if one reads Blake carefully in chronological order, the level of difficulty rises at a pace more or less in step with one's growing comprehension of his characteristic symbols, situations and rhetorical tactics, as if Blake was arranging a *gradus ad Parnassum* for those who would follow his path, the '*Children of the future Age, | Reading this indignant page*' ('A Little Girl Lost') whom he wants to teach and delight.

For Blake was well aware that most people found his work difficult. 'You say that I want somebody to Elucidate my Ideas,' he wrote to a discontented patron in 1799. 'But you ought to know that What is Grand is necessarily obscure to Weak men. That which can be made Explicit to the Idiot is not worth my care. The wisest of the Ancients considered what is not too Explicit as the fittest for Instruction because it rouzes the faculties to act. I name Moses Solomon Esop Homer Plato' (E 702). Blake can certainly make most readers, even experienced readers, feel at times like weak idiots, but he can also make them feel like giants released from chains. When they sense something grand behind the obscurities, something energetic, prolific and wise, it may rouse their faculties to act, it may awaken the slumbering power that Blake called the 'Real Self' or the Imagination. Like no other poet I know, Blake affords a heady pleasure in solving intriguing puzzles at the same time as a visceral and sometimes staggering sensation of discovering strange and vital truth.

Blake is unique in another way. Although he is honoured today mainly for his poetry, he was known in his day, spent most of his time and earned most of his income as an engraver and painter. Commissioned by book publishers, he engraved sets of illustrations for de luxe editions of popular poets; sometimes his designs were engraved by others (to his chagrin), and sometimes he engraved others' designs (which he found equally frustrating). He painted sets of large watercolours for a few patrons. His living was always meagre, though he worked every day of his life, his wife Catherine often beside him in his studio, colouring his copperplate designs or helping in some other way. Though he must have known it would bring him little income, he invested immense amounts of time and imaginative energy into what we now call his 'illuminated' poems. These are composite works of design and text, etched on the same plate and coloured by hand. All his published poems except *Poetical Sketches* (printed but not sold) and *The French Revolution* (set up in type but not printed) were 'published' in this way, and if you wanted to buy a copy you would have to walk over to his studio, examine the sample, place an order and come back a few weeks or months later.

Seldom does one of Blake's designs 'illustrate' the accompanying text in any familiar sense, and seldom can you find a line in the text that might be a 'caption' to the design. Sometimes the design seems to illustrate a text on another page or on no page at all, sometimes it seems to embody a symbolic or allegorical dimension that the text only suggests. Often the design is so prominent and interesting that it acquires a semantic weight equal to the text's, with the result that the reader feels invited somehow to read them both, simultaneously, or back and forth, adjusting the meaning of each in the light of the other until a joint meaning emerges. Nor is this all. The words themselves make part of the design, as letters in titles turn into flowers or flames, children climb over them and birds fly in and out; and elsewhere letters lean forward italicized as if into the future or stand in chiselled Roman uprightness as if on a tombstone. Tiny flying and crawling things lurk amidst the lines below, tendrils and volutes and non-representational squiggles divide lines and fill empty spaces. Some critics claim that the spatial arrangements of the words create internal eye-rhymes, quasi-anagrams and more complex semantic interferences. The punctuation seems entirely arbitrary and some readers ignore it, but it can be rhetorically expressive, and to 'normalize' it as some editions do is sometimes to mislead.

Because they were coloured and bound by hand, no two copies of any work are identical. Of the twenty-one known copies of the *Songs of Innocence*, no two copies have the same order of plates, and of the twenty-eight copies of the combined *Innocence* and *Experience*, only the last few copies Blake produced follow a common order. Strictly speaking, then, each copy of each poem is a unique work of art, differing in its total effect from the other copies in ways often very difficult to articulate. Finally, there are reports that Blake would sing some of his 'songs' to friends: 'His tunes were sometimes most singularly beautiful, and were noted down by musical professors' (in the words of J. T. Smith). Blake apparently had not learnt musical notation, and no notes of the 'professors' have turned up, but we should keep in mind that for some of the shorter poems, at least, what has come down to us is a two-dimensional transcript (verbal and visual) of a 'total', or at least three-dimensional, work of art.

No one but a devoted Blakean with a large travel budget and nothing else to do can hope to look at more than a few copies of Blake's poems. Recently, however, inexpensive colour facsimiles of several works have appeared, and collections of his writings now often include a few plates or black-and-white figures. (See the Further Reading section at the end of this book.) The present study includes no designs, so readers who possess unillustrated editions of Blake's work set in 'normal' type should try to spend time with facsimiles. The discussions that follow, however, will not assume that adequate facsimiles are at hand but will dwell disproportionately on the texts. For generations of readers who have known Blake through conventionally printed anthologies, Blake's poetry, however obscure, has not seemed incomplete or unsatisfying. Having discovered Blake's work in normal type when I was a university student and grown to love it, I was amazed when I learned that all those wonderful poems and prose visions came originally with pictures, and yet when I finally saw them I was sometimes disappointed. Many of them were as wonderful as the texts, 'but others seemed only to limit my imagination. Some connoisseurs of art, on the other hand, find the texts to be disappointing detractions from the splendour of the designs. Certainly it is most respectful of Blake's intention and of the original objects themselves to approach them as composite works, but I don't think Blake would mind if we learned to read his words first. Indeed the evidence from the notebook drafts suggests he revised his poems with an eye to such things as the coherence, compression and completeness of the texts by themselves, whatever designs might have been hovering overhead as he laboured on them.

When Blake was born on 28 November 1757, in London, George II was still king, the largely rural population of England and Wales was about 6.5 million, and the Industrial Revolution was scarcely imaginable, although the preconditions for it (growing population and demand for goods, agricultural surplus, technological innovations) were certainly established. When he died not quite seventy years later, on 12

August 1827, the number of people in England and Wales had more than doubled and the Industrial Revolution had progressed well past irreversible 'take-off': cotton textiles, for example, an almost negligible product in 1757 (compared to woollen goods), had grown by 1827 to command half the value of all domestically produced exports and employed an army of weavers on perhaps 50,000 looms powered by steam. London's population had grown faster than the national average and now approached 2 million, making it by far the largest city in Europe. It was not the industrial centre (Blake never visited the new industrial cities of the north), but it was the European hub of commerce and banking and the heart of a global empire.

Blake was seventeen when he heard about the battles of Lexington and Concord, and thirty-one when the Bastille was taken in Paris. The American and French Revolutions engaged his imagination and set it on a course from which in certain essentials it never wandered. But during over half of his lifetime England was at war, and at war with the revolutionary countries he admired. The 'moral subversion' of young people that Wordsworth blamed on England's reactionary policy towards France affected the somewhat older Blake as well, and his bitterness was deepened by oppression at home – the sights all around him of hunger and disease, vagabonds and harlots, boys sold into servitude to chimney-sweep masters or drafted into the army to fight other boys from France, and imaginative engravers and poets neglected by the 'hirelings' that dominated the book trade and academies. Those who knew him, however, called him a happy man, continually in converse with spiritual beings, serenely detached from earthly woes. The evidence of his works is less one-sided: he despaired, and struggled against despair, sometimes triumphantly, through much of his life.

Blake was the second of five children born to James Blake, a hosier, and his wife Catherine. As a child he saw visions and showed artistic skill, so he was sent to a drawing school and then, in 1772, apprenticed for seven years to James Basire, engraver to the London Society of Antiquaries, where he learned his craft as well as acquiring some of his political and poetical opinions. (The Society took an interest in republican ideas and revered John Milton.) In 1779 he began studying at the Royal Academy and within a year began exhibiting pictures there, often with historical themes. At twenty-four he married Catherine Boucher, five years younger than he was and illiterate; he taught her to read, write, make prints and colour. They never had children, but Blake was devoted to his brother Robert, ten years younger, taught him drawing and nursed him when he caught tuberculosis until his death, at nineteen, in 1787. Thereafter he communicated with Robert 'in the Spirit' and even claimed to learn new techniques from him; in his prophetic epic *Milton*, which has much to do with brotherhood, Blake engraved two full-page, mirror-image designs of 'William' and 'Robert' receiving inspiration from on high.

The most important of Blake's technical inventions, on which he said Robert helped him, was relief etching. He called it 'illuminated printing' and claimed in a prospectus of 1793 that it is 'a style more ornamental, uniform, and grand, than any before discovered', and 'combines the Painter and the Poet'. The opposite of intaglio, which is the method of incising or sinking a design (or text) into a plate, relief etching lowers the level of the plate everywhere else so the design stands out. We are not sure how Blake transferred his designs on to the copper plate, assuming he worked them out first on paper, but what appeared on the plate (back to front, of course) was a design in an impervious substance called a 'resist' or 'ground', probably a wax or tar. He would then bathe the plate in acids that would eat away everything not covered by the 'resist'. In *The Marriage of Heaven and Hell* Blake called this 'printing in the infernal method, by corrosives, which in Hell are salutary and medicinal, melting apparent surfaces away, and displaying the infinite which was hid' (plate 14). It is much like Michelangelo's notion that a sculptor removes stone away in layers in order to reveal the figure hidden within. It became a fruitful metaphor for Blake's epistemology: against John Locke's model of a blank slate incised by experience, Blake claimed we are endowed with deep powers which experience only crusts over or represses. His job, as relief engraver and poet, was to cleanse away the incrustation and bring out what is buried inside us.

Blake made a modest but promising start as a poet (*Poetical Sketches* was printed, in normal type, in 1783 but distributed only privately), as a painter and as a book illustrator, but a print shop in which he was a partner failed. In 1789 he began attending meetings of the Swedenborgian Society, inspired by the writings of the Swedish scientist and mystical Bible commentator Emanuel Swedenborg (1688–1772), but within a year he broke with it; *The Marriage of Heaven and Hell*, which he finished engraving in 1792, is among other things a brilliant parody of Swedenborg's writings. Having illustrated books for the publisher Joseph Johnson since 1780, Blake met several of the prominent radicals in the Johnson circle, including Thomas Paine, William Godwin and Mary Wollstonecraft (whose *Original Stories from Real Life* he illustrated). Between 1789 and 1795 Blake began a series of poems and designs in his 'illuminated printing' that constitute his greatest achievement: *Songs of Innocence, The Book of Thel, Visions of the Daughters of Albion, America: A Prophecy, Songs of Innocence and of Experience, Europe: A Prophecy, The Book of Urizen, The Song of Los, The Book of Los* and *The Book of Ahania.* Of these only a few of the short songs became widely known; of the longer poems at most a score of copies have survived, and not many more of them were produced or sold. A very ambitious book-illustration project followed – 537 watercolour drawings for Edward Young's popular *Night Thoughts* (1742), of which forty-three were engraved – but within a year Blake had no commissions for books, only a handful of patrons and friends (among them the artists Flaxman and Fuseli) and little reputation either as poet or as painter.

At this point (1800) Blake responded to William Hayley's invitation to move near him in Sussex, where he could work on commissions Hayley arranged. He enjoyed what he called his 'three-years' slumber' in Felpham in some ways, but the work was uninspiring, he had a quarrel with Hayley (obscurely recounted in the 'Bard's Song' of *Milton*), and a drunken soldier named Schofield accused him of seditious utterances against the king. Blake was acquitted (1804), but the experience can only have deepened the political bitterness he had felt for years. *Milton* and *Jerusalem*, his two completed epics, are both dated 1804 but took many years to engrave; the latter draws on the manuscript of *Vala* or *The Four Zoas*, which has survived. He found a few more book commissions and patrons for watercolours and oils, but he also felt tricked by engravers and publishers and deliberately ignored or unfairly ridiculed by reviewers. Late in life, however, he found himself at the centre of an admiring group of young painters, who included Samuel Palmer and Edward Calvert. His last major projects were his designs for the Book of Job, which integrate pictures with quotations to make a visionary interpretation of the book, and his one hundred watercolours for Dante's *Divine Comedy*. He died aged sixty-nine, singing, it is reported, of the sights of heaven. Four years later Catherine died, also aged sixty-nine.

1. *Songs of Innocence*

As the Piper in the 'Introduction' leads us to expect, the world of the *Songs of Innocence* is a world of lambs. There are real lambs followed by watchful shepherds and addressed by little children, and there are metaphorical lambs, the children themselves. The orphans of London are 'multitudes of lambs', Tom Dacre's head is 'curl'd like a lambs back', and the black boy and white boy 'like lambs ... [will] joy' around the 'tent of God', their Shepherd. There are metaphorical shepherds for the children – mothers, nurses, 'Old John', 'wise guardians of the poor' and angels – and there are even metaphorical shepherds for the lost 'emmets' (ants). There are beetles for the emmets and beadles for the orphans. It is a world of caring and concern and of ultimate protectedness. Even where things go wrong, and children wander lost or end up orphans or slaves or 'chimney sweepers' or are pounced upon by dreadful wolves and 'tygers', a guardian from a higher realm intervenes and sets things right, in the next world if not in this.

Even a first reading of the *Songs* shows us that the imagined little world of the infant, protected by its mother from every fear and want, or of those lucky children whose worst experience is to be summoned home before they are ready to go, or to dream about a forlorn insect, is no different from the larger world of the older children who have suffered, of the mother who weeps while singing a lullaby, or of the speaker of 'Holy Thursday', an adult on-looker at the procession of orphans. The world of innocence is a child's world, and it is preserved in the minds of full-grown children by projecting the memory or desire for parental protection on to a higher realm. The adults in turn teach their faith in heavenly guardians to their children, who imagine the heavenly guardians as just like their parents. It is a world of pious Christianity, and Blake presents it in perhaps its most charming, subtle and tender form. Blake sees through it, and wants us to see through it, but he does not despise it, or the people who believe in it. Indeed, as we shall see, Blake believes in a version of it himself.

He also expects us, I think, to travel through the world of innocence poem by poem, and picture by picture, with imaginative openness. He does not state explicitly the limitations of this world. If as adults we bring a condescending scepticism to the confined and fragile little

1

songs, he invites us, as Jesus did, to become a child again. If we come as grown-up innocents, already convinced that God protects the world's lambs, he shows us gently, by example rather than precept, how beliefs like ours are inculcated in us by our priests and social betters. 'Innocence' and 'innocent', then, are richly interesting words. The lambs with their 'innocent call', the orphans with their 'innocent faces', are innocent in that they have done no harm, of course, but they are also innocent in that they have experienced no harm, or at least nothing that challenges their faith; they are naïve and vulnerable to the machinations of the experienced world, and yet superior to it in their blessed simplicity. The same is true of the adult narrators.

The Piper

If 'innocence' deserves pondering, so does the 'of' in *Songs of Innocence*. For these seem to be songs not only *about* innocence but *by* innocence as well, no matter what the apparent age of their speaker (or singer). They *belong to* innocence in a manner indifferent to distinctions between subject and object, between the song's singer and the song's theme; the songs are 'of' innocence in the way the Piper's songs are 'songs of pleasant glee' and 'happy chear'. They are of the world of innocence, too, because their internal audience consists of innocents. We may suspect that the *Songs of Innocence* is 'really' aimed at sophisticated adults, but we may be 'really' children anyway, as we have just noted, and we should take seriously the Piper's story that this book owes its existence to the demands of a child, even if he is an imaginary one on a cloud.

The 'Introduction', in fact, admirably introduces the songs that follow, and the reader should dwell on it longer than he or she might do for its own sake. It is first of all a little story, told in a childlike, concatenary way, one event after another as it takes place, like the more complex stories of (by and about) the Little Black Boy and the Chimney Sweeper. The child makes demands, 'so' the Piper responds – four demands followed by four responses beginning with 'so':

> Pipe a song about a Lamb;
> So I piped with merry chear[.]

It ends with a string of 'ands' as the Piper gets to work preparing his tools and writing. The fourth 'so', however, is oddly placed:

2

> Piper sit thee down and write
> In a book that all may read –
> So he vanish'd from my sight.
> And I pluck'd a hollow reed.

We would expect '*And* he vanish'd ... *So* I pluck'd', but the Piper seems so caught up in the game-like pattern the child has imposed on him that he forgets who is responding to whom. They have become one: the child may vanish from the Piper's sight because the Piper has internalized him. (It is also true that the Piper's audience of one must now yield to an audience of many, to the 'Every child' of the final line.)

Piper and child have been united in spirit all along, of course. The Piper plays some songs of pleasant glee and immediately finds a child laughing; we might imagine that the song that caused the child to materialize was the 'Laughing Song' with its refrain of 'Ha, Ha, He', the child on the cloud being an embodiment of 'the air [that] does laugh with our merry wit'. He wants a song about a lamb, so the Piper *pipes* one, and it is so successful that he must repeat it, and the child weeps (with joy) to hear it. The child is stirred by the tune alone. Has the child learned the words beforehand? (Presumably not, for he tells the Piper to publish them.) Does he divine the words from the tune? Is the tune so expressive in itself that it imparts what the words convey? We again get the suggestion that the child is a projection of the Piper, an inspiration from the air around him. But the prompt and cheerful obedience of the Piper presages the ready responsiveness and empathy of just about every being in Creation to every other being in the rest of the *Songs*. Lambs call and ewes reply in 'The Shepherd'; the skies are made happy by the sun, while the bells welcome the spring and inspire the birds to sing louder in 'The Echoing Green'; the 'Little Black Boy' dreams of the day when he will shade the English boy from the sun and stroke his hair; the 'Chimney Sweeper' sees little Tom Dacre crying, 'so' he instantly responds with consoling words. 'On Anothers Sorrow' culminates this theme (Blake placed it last in the book more often than any other song, though in several copies he placed it in the middle); it is precisely *about* instant and unselfconscious compassion:

> Can I see anothers woe,
> And not be in sorrow too.
> Can I see anothers grief,
> And not seek for kind relief.

If we can fully enter into the spirit of the Piper's introduction, we are ready to appreciate all the songs that follow.

The title-page of the original edition makes clear that 'The Author & Printer' is 'W Blake', while the 'Introduction' invites us to regard all the songs as written by the Piper. The frontispiece makes clear that the Piper is a shepherd, as we might have guessed from his repertory of 'lamb' songs and the fact that in over half the copies 'The Shepherd' immediately follows the 'Introduction'. We are in a pastoral world, with many of the props and themes of the classical pastoral tradition, such as the pipe and the hollow reed, the sweet lot of the shepherd and the pleasant sounds of nature. Samuel Johnson hoped he had put an end to pastoral poetry, and Blake was certainly aware that the last century had been glutted with tedious imitations of Theocritus and Virgil, but he none the less cheerfully courts ridicule with another batch of poems in this genre, perhaps in the belief that the form of a children's book would insulate them from adult contempt. He does have a fresh turn or two to make in the pastoral conventions, however. It is a clever conceit (though whether it is entirely original in Blake's work I cannot say) to manufacture a 'rural pen' out of a hollow reed, rather than to pluck one from a bird, for it is a routine pastoral fact that *pipes* are made of hollow reeds; the pen is thus a transformed pipe. To bring up pens and writing at all is interesting because it is unnecessary: for centuries readers had accepted the pretence that all written works, even epics and plays, were songs. Blake's songs, moreover, were really songs, and if the reports are right, his tunes affected his hearers almost as much as the Piper's affected his. But Blake's songs were also, and very importantly, illuminated texts, and the pretence that one can sing multi-coloured pictures may have seemed too much to maintain.

Some readers have hesitated over 'stain'd' in the last stanza.

> And I made a rural pen,
> And I stain'd the water clear,
> And I wrote my happy songs
> Every child may joy to hear.

'Clear' suggests 'innocent' or 'happy', and to stain clear water is symbolically to corrupt innocence, water being as clear and fluid as the air or cloud which are home to the child. Yet 'stain'd' in one context may have moral connotations, while in another it may not. In church, for instance, are we troubled by the thought of stained-glass windows? One critic thinks the Piper is attempting the impossible task of writing *on* water, but of course he is not: he is using water to make ink for his pen. Another critic suggests that to write, as opposed to piping or singing, is to limit or constrain the expressive freedom the poem ostensibly celebrates; writing is seen as a corruption of culture. But surely writing is the only way to go public, 'that all may read', and the very emblem of expressive spontaneity – the child on the cloud – insists upon it.

I mention these supposed shadows and ambiguities here because, if some recent critics are to be believed, Blake is filled with secondary and tertiary counter-meanings that lurk like quicksand or trapdoors underfoot, and an innocent reader of Blake must learn from experience to tread tiptoe through the primary level (which turns out not to be primary after all) and to leap and dance along all the others. For example, line 2 of 'The Shepherd' contains an allegedly ambiguous word:

> How sweet is the Shepherds sweet lot,
> From the morn to the evening he strays[.]

The shepherd, who should be looking for stray sheep, has gone astray himself, it might be argued. Watchful shepherd, watch thyself! Can we trust what he says and does? This subversive thought breeds others: is he a wolf in shepherd's clothing? And just what are shepherds, anyway? Aren't they authoritarians, like bishops, carrying long sticks, to confine us in folds or stampede us into doing what they want? And so on.

This sort of interpretation cannot be ruled out in advance, and the 'ambiguities' of every poem have to be considered case by case. The examples we have looked at are not very difficult to assess, and most readers will have the critical tact or judgement not to be misled by 'strays' unless lupine critics talk them into it. But how does one acquire this tact or judgement, and what are its principles? One way to acquire it, in fact the Blakean way, is negatively: to plunge through some of these supposed verbal trapdoors and follow all their ramifying tunnels and subsidiary trapdoors until the whole structure is undermined or deconstructed. But you must be thorough. All the connoisseurs of ambiguity I have read have been faint-hearted. They go just a little farther than previous readers. They take a step or two beyond the rug they have all been walking along so that they can pull it out from under the others; sometimes they manage even to pull it out from under themselves, and they all take an exhilarating bounce or two. But then they quite arbitrarily stop. They may feel they have made their point – that the surface level of the poem conceals dark anti-meanings – yet instead they find they have a tiger by the tail but not the courage to hang on. As a result their whole argument collapses and they do not possess judgement or tact, principles or methods, to prevent it.

In the 'Introduction', for example, the first line tells us the Piper is in 'the valleys wild'. In a valley you cannot see as far as you can on a hill: doesn't that imply the Piper lacks vision? It is 'wild': is he then like Dante at the opening of the *Inferno*, lost in a savage wood? Why does he bring tame sheep to this wild place? His songs are pleasant, but 'glee' has secondary meanings, which become primary when the whole poem is viewed more darkly. It can mean 'scornful jesting' or 'mockery': is he mocking the reader? It can mean (in northern English) 'squint', 'glance', 'sidelook': is he partly blind? Is he shifty, nervous, duplicitous? If you go persistently through the poem in this way, like a detective collecting clues, you will produce strange and disturbing readings, such as a sinister Pied Piper leading children to lose their innocence, or a blind and silly shepherd leading blind and sillier sheep into a 'rural pen', or a 'hollow' poem from which all inspiration has vanished, and you may proceed in this way until doomsday. In the end, you are left with an infinite number of arbitrary readings and no basis on which to choose among them. Is that what you want? If not, then you have taken the negative way towards wisdom. 'If the fool would persist in his folly he would become wise', wrote Blake in his 'Proverbs of Hell', and 'The road of excess leads to the palace of wisdom.'

This book will assume, as most readers and critics have always assumed until recently, that interpretation is possible, that there are principles for eliminating all but one or a small number of readings in nearly all cases, and that these principles have to do with linguistic probabilities, historical horizons, and conventions of speaking, construing speech and reading. One of the principles is coherence: a meaning of a word or phrase is more likely if it 'belongs' or fits with the other words and phrases around it, and this in turn is a matter of common linguistic usage, though it will often entail a little research into what the words meant in Blake's day. This principle does not assume in advance that a poem will be a tight 'organic' unity; like Occam's Razor, it takes the category of unity that eliminates unnecessary entities as a condition of rational thought. It does not preclude contradictions or inconsistencies in a poem, but it puts the burden of proof on them. While it is wary of ambiguities, it welcomes multiple meanings (such as those of allegory, symbolism and irony), for they do not conflict with coherence and indeed sometimes provide it. Relying on conventions, finally, does not blind us to Blake's, or any poet's, originality; indeed it enables us to see it, for an original poet relies on conventions in order to break them, or rather an original poet relies on many conventions in order to break a few of them. It is also possible that Blake broke so many, so often, especially in his later poetry and designs, that some passages will remain forever obscure, but knowing how much he has yielded to patient and imaginative exploration encourages us to keep at it, and no one wants to look foolish for prematurely pronouncing something impossible.

Jesus

More important than classical pastoral in the *Songs of Innocence* is Christian pastoral. The tradition that Jesus is the Good Shepherd and Christians are his flock is so familiar that we scarcely notice a metaphor in the 'pastor' of a 'congregation', or an emblem in the bishop's crozier or crook. But Blake brings it gently to life in the last two lines of 'The Shepherd':

> He is watchful while they [the sheep] are in peace,
> For they know when their Shepherd is nigh.

If there were no Good Shepherd tradition the poem would still make perfect sense, but in placing 'Shepherd' at the end Blake subtly evokes the thought that there may be another, divine Shepherd nigh and that the second 'they' includes the mortal shepherd with his sheep. (That Blake capitalizes 'Shepherd' both times is suggestive, but his practice is too erratic to rely on.) This thought clarifies the last line of the first stanza – 'And his tongue shall be filled with praise' – for we may have wondered whom he is praising. His sheep? No, he is praising the Good Shepherd, or Whoever it is that unites ewes and lambs and brings peace to the flock.

Even more central to Christian tradition, however, is the inverse metaphor that Jesus is the Lamb of God, an innocent lamb 'without blemish', acceptable to God as a sacrifice for our sins. In Blake, as in many writers before him, the identification of Jesus as Lamb is connected to the Incarnation and the Nativity, the arrival of the divine among us not only in human form but as a baby, born among common people and among animals. The child who asks the lamb 'who made thee' (in 'The Lamb') answers his own question and tells it how the three of them – lamb, child and Jesus – are all connected:

> He is called by thy name,
> For he calls himself a Lamb:

> He is meek & he is mild,
> He became a little child:
> I a child & thou a lamb,
> We are called by his name.

But Jesus grew to be a man and made the supreme sacrifice at his crucifixion – that is, after all, why he is called a lamb – and in doing so embraced us all again in our sorrows and death as well as in our joys and life. The speaker of 'On Anothers Sorrow' includes both aspects:

> He doth give his joy to all.
> He becomes an infant small.
> He becomes a man of woe
> He doth feel the sorrow too.
>
> . . . .
>
> O! he gives to us his joy,
> That our grief he may destroy
> Till our grief is fled & gone
> He doth sit by us and moan[.]

There is a great deal of grief in Blake's world of innocence; most of the tears are not tears of joy. The mother's 'Cradle Song' tells of unaccountable tears – 'Sleep sleep, happy sleep / While o'er thee thy mother weep' – perhaps over all the griefs the child will have undergone as she foresees it, in Yeats's words, with sixty or more winters on its head, and then the song remarkably combines into one image the infant Jesus, the Man of Sorrows, her own tears and her weeping baby:

> Sweet babe in thy face
> Holy image I can trace.
> Sweet babe once like thee,
> Thy maker lay and wept for me[.]

In 'The Divine Image' people pray in their distress and even the robin in 'The Blossom' seems to have something to sob over, though both human and bird find consolation. In several poems, however, conditions seem so bad that this world as a whole is seen as needing the recompense of another. Two such poems, 'The Little Black Boy' and 'The Chimney Sweeper', we shall turn to shortly; first we should briefly consider 'Night', which states very bluntly the possible evils of this life which have only a transcendent cure.

Spoken by a shepherd who is going home for the night, the poem describes the loving care of nocturnal angels who pour blessing and joy on all creatures. Those they find weeping they put to sleep, as mothers do their children, by singing lullabies. But

When wolves and tygers howl for prey
They pitying stand and weep;
Seeking to drive their thirst away,
And keep them from the sheep.

Humans are susceptible to pity, to tears. Blake was later to write that 'a Tear is an Intellectual thing; / And a Sigh is the Sword of an Angel King' (*Jerusalem,* plate 52, lines 25–6). In this world, however, at least in this poem, beasts of prey are sometimes impervious to such weapons.

But if they rush dreadful;
The angels most heedful,
Recieve each mild spirit,
New worlds to inherit.

The sheep are killed, but they go to heaven. There they find what they never found in this life, a lion lying down with a lamb. On earth the lion would not respond to the pitying gestures of the angels, but in heaven

the lions ruddy eyes,
Shall flow with tears of gold:
And pitying the tender cries,

it will become a shepherd itself and guard the fold. It will even become a lamb, or at least a herbivore, and 'Graze after thee and weep'.

Blake widens the world of innocence, then, to embrace the ultimate in suffering, but he also keeps it 'innocent', and rather obviously so. Where the mutual love and concern that are so richly embodied in the songs break down – blossoms and robins find no warm bosoms as they usually do, boys lost in the lonely fen are not found by God or their fathers and chimney sweepers die in their black chimneys – there an angel intervenes and escorts the victim to a world where the broken ties of love and pity are reknit for ever.

To return for the last time to the 'Introduction', we may ask if our knowledge of the poems that follow alters our reading, or re-reading, of the piper and his story. We have seen a great deal of weeping. (Blake lived in what has been called the 'Age of Sensibility', when real people of both sexes wept more often and more openly than they do now, and so did literary characters.) Are we to take the child's response to the second piping of the song – 'he wept to hear' – as a sorrowful one, as if he knows that the subject of the 'song about a Lamb' is the Lamb of God who suffered on the cross? Is the child the infant Jesus himself? It is pretty clear (on the principle of coherence if nothing else) that the

9

weeping is 'for joy', as it is explicitly said to be after the Piper finally sings the song, for the child has been laughing and the music is full of glee and cheer. But then, why *do* people weep for joy? Surely the child is not in that state of helpless convulsive laughter that (in real life) brings tears to the eyes as the laugher gasps for breath. It seems equally unlikely that he is weeping because the joy has brought relief from sadness or anxiety, for what has this child experienced yet? It is hard to shake off altogether a vague premonitory hint of grief when we are aware of the poems that follow. And surely there is some sense in which the child on the cloud is Jesus, for all children are Jesus, we have learned, and Jesus is in us all or near us all, especially when we are childlike. Blake later explicitly identified Jesus with the imagination, which he identified in turn with the Holy Spirit, that aspect of God which remains with us after the death of the historical Jesus and brings us together in the Church. The world of innocence, in fact, would be well described as a Church, where each member of the flock is a shepherd by turns, brother or sister to each other in their joys and woes. The child on the cloud, with his instantaneous responsiveness to the Piper, is an emblem of the reciprocal love that constitutes the Holy Spirit and its Church.

I think we can go that far, but interesting questions of method hover about such extensions of meaning. Some of the most impressive and influential Blake interpreters, such as Northrop Frye, read every poem in the context of every other poem, or against the backdrop of the entire Blakean 'system' as it unfolds in the years following the *Songs of Innocence.* With this approach, a 'tyger' that 'rushes dreadful' is really an 'animal form of wisdom', and the state of innocence itself is to be comprehended under the later category of Beulah, which is the third of four levels of imaginative power. It is certainly true that after the difficult but fascinating effort of mastering Blake's unique mythopoeic world, with Orc and Urizen and spectres and emanations, the earlier poems may look interestingly different. A new reading, with eyes tutored by *Jerusalem,* may show us aspects we missed when we read them 'innocently'. But it may also lead us to impose meanings that are not 'there', and we should remember, as experienced Blakeans, that Blake's 'experienced' characters are often blinkered.

The question may resolve itself into another: what is the work of art we are considering? Blake 'published' his works; that is, he engraved and sold them separately, and only a few of them, such as *America* and *Europe,* are tied to each other. And he did not wait to sell his earlier works, of course, until he finished the later ones, if he even had them in mind. On the other hand, even in an early work such as *The Book of Thel* (dated, like *Innocence,* 1789) we find a name or two whose reference is doubtful in the work itself but whose character and history are fully presented in later works. The systematic interpreters of Blake have been called the 'one-big-poem' school, for they seem to take as a single work the complete corpus of his writings, sometimes even including his unfinished manuscripts, his letters and the marginal notes he wrote in books that he read; some scholars now include all his graphic works as well in one immense whole. This seems to me a mistake, not only because it breeds misreadings and obliterates real inconsistencies, but also because it rests on a circular argument: by positing Blake's *œuvre* as one complete work it invokes the principle of coherence across and among poems, and having found unities everywhere it then justifies taking the works as one. Yet if a character with the same name appears in two or more poems, it does not follow that it must be the 'same' character in each, that his or her action or character is continuous across the poems. While it is true that the skills we gain in working through one poem will serve us well in the next, and that many Blakean terms and ideas will recur, often verbatim, from poem to poem, we should try to test our knowledge and expectations against each new work with an open mind.

We should remember, too, that no two copies of the *Songs of Innocence* or of the joint *Songs of Innocence and of Experience* are identical – either the order of poems changes (with occasional omissions, moreover) or the colouring of the designs or both – so it is a nice question which is the definitive work of art. If we take the work as the family of similar books, then it is difficult to resist the conclusion that the order and even the colouring are not very important, and that we should give greatest weight to the individual poems and essential designs (though some striking differences in colouring will sometimes give us pause) and to the 'world' they build up.

Blake's Critique of Religion

Let us turn to the two most poignantly powerful of the *Songs of Innocence,* 'The Little Black Boy' and 'The Chimney Sweeper'. They are twin poems spoken by spiritual twins, boys black by birth or occupation, semi-orphaned and now separated from their surviving parents (the black boy's father is never mentioned and the boy now seems to be in England, perhaps as a slave, certainly as a servant). They both preserve a great capacity for loving other children despite their difficult lives and the oppressive conventional versions of Christianity they have been taught. They both recite their own poems, as if Blake has brought them to us and asked them to tell us their stories. They wonderfully rouse our sympathy and admiration while showing how religion has cramped their otherwise beautiful imaginations.

The black boy states his basic notions about racial differences in the opening stanza before telling how he learned them from his mother.

> My mother bore me in the southern wild,
> And I am black, but O! my soul is white;
> White as an angel is the English child:
> But I am black as if bereav'd of light.

Truth and error are so intimately confused here that one hesitates to analyse them, just as we might refrain from re-educating the black boy if we met him lest we disrupt the precarious but consoling adaptation of his beliefs to his life. His soul is indeed white, if goodness and candour are white, but in this boy's mind the moral meaning of colours is not limited to souls. A soul may be white as an angel but a soul is invisible; it is the English child's skin that is white. Goodness is implied, yet the black boy knows nothing about the white boy's soul, and indeed we might infer from his loneliness that no white boy has deigned to befriend him. When he thinks of his own black skin as bereaved of light he has again confused soul with body, for it is his soul that is bereaved of light, in the sense that he is not enlightened enough to think his way through the prejudices of his mother and the English people he lives among; yet his soul is also filled with light, an inner light, or at least an inner heat, a generous love. Bodies, in any case, are not bereaved of light: the phrase belongs to theological tales about fallen angels who have become black devils by rebelling against the light of God. If on the other hand we take 'light' literally here, he is precisely wrong about skin colour, as it is the English boy, living in foggy England, who lacks sunlight; the black boy is sunburnt, as his mother has explained.

But she has also explained that a body is only a cloud, or a grove of trees.

> And we are put on earth a little space,
> That we may learn to bear the beams of love,
> And these black bodies and this sun-burnt face
> Is but a cloud, and like a shady grove.

The cloud-body or grove-body, like the grove they are sitting under this morning, protects the soul from the intense beams of love sent down from God, who lives in the sun. This supernal male God, she has explained, is generous and loving, for he gives away his light and heat to the flowers, trees, beasts and men, bringing them comfort and joy. He is transcendent, like God the Father, but also immanent, like Jesus and the Holy Spirit (whom St John calls the Comforter), for his light and heat permeate our world. (We get a hint here as to why white is good, for at night, when it is dark, God must be absent.) We will not try to sort out the meanings of transcendence and immanence, which permeate Blake's own beliefs and most Christian theology as well as the boy's beliefs, but it seems clear that what the heavenly Father sends down, though gently shaded by the mother, is a harsh and dreadful love, scorching beams we never learn to bear until our little space in this vale of tears is concluded, or to be exact, when we learn to bear it, we die and go to heaven.

> For when our souls have learn'd the heat to bear
> The cloud will vanish we shall hear his voice.

Noting the two meanings of 'bear', we could take this as saying that when we learn to bring love, and not just to endure it, we are in heaven, wherever it may be. But the mother's story implies a world of suffering beyond anything that an English child, reading this poem, is likely to have experienced – unless, of course, he is a chimney sweeper or orphan.

The black boy, in any case, has imbibed the dualism of his mother and now looks forward to the day when he shall come out from his shady grove and rise free of his black cloud, to where he shall not only encounter God the Father – remembering that he seems to have no earthly father – but meet the English boy who will finally love him. There, if he understands what his mother taught him, he ought to expect perfect equality with the white boy, for they are both free of their clouds, but the best he can imagine is a loving subaltern role, a little like that of a valet, and an assimilation of his nature to his superior's.

> Ill shade him from the heat till he can bear,
> To lean in joy upon our fathers knee.
> And then I'll stand and stroke his silver hair,
> And be like him and he will then love me.

If the English boy has shed his cloud-body he will not need shading from the heat, or if for some reason new soul-clouds are needed for protection in heaven, the black boy is no better equipped than the white. And since the black boy has learned, at least in his body, to bear the heat of love on earth, if anyone must come to be 'like' the other, it should be the English boy who comes to learn the love the black boy already knows. This is, in fact, the radical truth in the poem, truer than the black boy can comprehend. He seems to intuit a unity of body and soul, as if the Pauline notion of the 'spiritual body', absent from his mother's teaching, lurks in his imagination: bodies will be resurrected too. But alas, in the black boy's vision, so will skin colour and the social values attached to it.

Blake may well have known the black poet Phillis Wheatley's book, *Poems on Various Subjects,* which appeared in London in 1773, for his black boy, except for these confused radical intuitions, shares her unenlightened version of Christianity.

> 'Twas mercy brought me from my pagan land,
> Taught my benighted soul to understand
> That there's a God, that there's a Savior too:
> Once I redemption neither sought nor knew.
> Some view our sable race with scornful eye,
> 'Their color is a diabolic dye.'
> Remember, Christians, Negroes, black as Cain,
> May be refined, and join the angelic train.

In his 'Song of Liberty' Blake grants that blacks need enlightening – 'O African! black African! (go. winged thought widen his forehead.)' – but they need it no more than Asians or Europeans, and they don't need refining. Yet Africa sometimes plays a redemptive role in Blake's grand historical vision: the most oppressed race will teach us how to love our fellow men and women.

The black boy having brought his clouded view of things with him to heaven, we wonder how Blake will colour the illustration of the two boys. The poem is distributed over two plates, and the second one shows the boys standing before Christ who is sitting under a willow tree (rather as the black mother is sitting under her tree in the preceding plate) and carrying a shepherd's crook; there are sheep in the background. The black boy is standing behind the white boy, as if he has introduced him to Christ; it has been suggested that the scene alludes to the pictorial tradition of the guardian angel presenting a human soul to God. And the colour of the boys? In some copies the black boy is just as light as the English boy; in others he is very black; in still others he is a shade or two darker. Blake seems to have felt caught in a dilemma. To paint the black boy black shows him still in the grip of the racist views he has learned on earth, even though he says he will be free of the black cloud when he is in heaven. To paint him white is to come closer to the 'real' equality of heaven and to acknowledge his point about leaving the cloud behind. But this is not the real heaven; it is the black boy's projection of it, the joint product of the maternal lessons and the ideological environment of England. And then why paint them both white? It would state the point more radically to make them both black. In short, there is no correct way to colour them. Blake can only tilt the emphasis subtly one way or the other, to a fuller fleshing out of the black boy's view or to an adumbration of the brotherhood the black boy could only wish for during his little space on earth.

One cannot help wishing the little black boy had met the Chimney Sweeper. Though he would have found no silver hair to stroke, he would have found a boy capable of returning love and solace. In the Chimney Sweeper's recital, he deals with his own life and its woes in one quatrain, almost as if it is a mere preliminary to the story he really wants to tell, the story of little Tom Dacre.

> When my mother died I was very young,
> And my father sold me while yet my tongue,
> Could scarcely cry weep weep weep weep.
> So your chimneys I sweep & in soot I sleep.
>
> Theres little Tom Dacre ...

The little tongue trying to say 'sweep' and crying 'weep' instead may appeal rather too obviously to our pity, but the appeal is so brief, the rest so matter-of-fact (the 'so', echoing the childlike logic of the 'Introduction', is poignant in its readiness to accept an outrageous social scandal), and there is so quick a transition to the other little boy, that our pity is all the more effectively touched. To little Tom, new at his task and crying over the loss of his white curls, the older boy offers the simple but almost paradoxical consolation that if he has no hair the soot cannot spoil it. That is enough to quiet him and prompt a dream where all is set right. An angel unlocks the boys from their black, chimney-like coffins.

> Then down a green plain leaping laughing they run
> And wash in a river and shine in the Sun.
>
> Then naked & white, all their bags left behind,
> They rise upon clouds, and sport in the wind.

If the coffins are chimneys, the bags are their bodies. Tom has absorbed the language of the Bible (baptism, the waters of life, the raiment of the sun) but is inflecting it with the concrete particulars of his life. It is as if he is reinventing Christianity out of his miserable condition. Blake seems to agree with Karl Marx here that religion is the sigh of the oppressed creature, and we see the oppression inscribed in certain details. How strange this heaven is that it must contain an angel to tell Tom to be a good boy. This heaven bears the scars not only of a boy who has lost (or never had) a mother or father, for nearly all the *Songs of Innocence* contain a maternal or paternal figure, but of one who has heard a great deal of officious advice from his master and other elders. The echo of 'be a good boy' will reverberate for all eternity.

The older sweeper also echoes it in his final line, the apparent moral of the story beginning with 'so'.

> And so Tom awoke and we rose in the dark
> And got with our bags & our brushes to work.
> Tho' the morning was cold, Tom was happy & warm,
> So if all do their duty, they need not fear harm.

'Do your duty' has left its mark on this line, as an equivalent to the phrase 'get to work', but 'duty' reverberates subtly with further meanings. Blake saw the function of religion, and of ideology in general, as to inculcate duty, to keep us at our tasks in the cold and the dark, and the older sweeper plays his part as an unwitting junior propagandist of the faith. But he has done his duty in a deeper sense: he has comforted the afflicted, he has forgotten himself in a simple loving response to a younger child in distress. That duty shines through the official one and appeals implicitly to us, the readers. Since the fourth line – 'your chimneys I sweep' – we have been quietly implicated in the suffering of these children, and if we are included in the 'all' of the final line then our duty is to emulate the sweeper and bring comfort to his brothers. We do that, however, not by telling bedtime stories to help them sleep, and even less by arguing them out of the religion that is their only hope, but by removing the terrible conditions that make their religion a necessity. To cite Marx again, 'The critique of religion is the critique in embryo of the vale of tears of which religion is the halo'.

At the time Blake wrote the poem a campaign was under way for Parliament to set minimum standards for the treatment of 'climbing boys', as the sweepers were known: they should not begin such work until they are eight, they should be washed once a week, and they should not be made to climb chimneys with fires in them. Years later, little more than that having been accomplished, a new campaign began, and Charles Lamb, who had long had an interest in Blake, sent 'The Chimney Sweeper' to an anthology published on the boys' behalf. He altered 'Tom Dacre' to 'Tom Toddy', thereby losing a possible allusion

16

to Dacre's Alms House on James Street, where sweep masters might find boys, or to the Greek word for 'tear', but he rightly called the poem 'the Flower of the set'. England did not do its duty, however, until 1875, when Parliament finally forbade sending boys into chimneys.

Shepherd heaven in 'Night' contains an herbivorous lion who guards the fold; black-boy heaven finds spiritually superior black boys still serving white boys; sweeper heaven has a bossy angel. As if he wants to show just how cramped and confined such heavens are, Blake allows only half an inch of space for the design of 'The Chimney Sweeper', no wider than a quatrain of text, at the bottom of the plate. An angel is releasing a boy from his coffin; ten other boys, already freed, are rejoicing, embracing or running for the river. It is hard to escape the feeling that this half-inch, as narrow as the chimneys the boys climb up and down every day, is just about all the room society has seen fit to give them. The miracle is that the boys manage to fill this tiny world with love, comfort, imagination and good cheer.

Before we leave the *Songs of Innocence* we should look briefly at a poem that stands a little apart from the others because its speaker seems to be an adult, and an adult with views that seem inadequate to their occasion. The irony that seems to play across it raises questions as to just what innocence is when it captivates a pious older observer. The speaker of 'Holy Thursday' is impressed by the sight of the annual procession of charity orphans into St Paul's Cathedral and by the sound of their choral songs. He sees how colourful their clothing is, compares them to flowers and to lambs, senses a 'radiance all their own', and in two climactic similes he tries to grasp something sublime in their singing.

> Now like a mighty wind they raise to heaven the voice of song
> Or like harmonious thunderings the seats of heaven among[.]

But he has also been noting another sort of thing. The children's faces are 'clean' (a word that appears nowhere else in *Innocence*), they walk 'two & two' behind 'Grey-headed beadles' carrying 'wands as white as snow', and they sit in companies inside the church. After the high point of the singing, which the speaker imagines has reached to the 'seats of heaven', he brings us down to earth in an unselfconscious, deadpan tone and then closes his account with a pious moral.

> Beneath them sit the aged men wise guardians of the poor
> Then cherish pity, lest you drive an angel from your door[.]

He seems entirely unaware of the tension between the colour, radiance

17

and spiritual power of the children and the cold, colourless severity of the guardians. No doubt the guardians sit physically beneath the children in St Paul's but, coming right after the seats of heaven, 'beneath them' resounds with moral or spiritual meanings truer than the speaker knows. That is also the case with the final line. The speaker may have cherished pity as he watched and listened, and he probably makes an annual contribution to one of the orphanages, but we get the feeling that it is precisely pity that he cherishes, and occasions for pity like this one, rather than the children themselves. 'The Divine Image' praises pity as one of the divine virtues and gives it 'a human face', but we suspect that our observer of poor orphans has abstracted pity from those clean faces he admires and, like the speaker of 'The Human Abstract' in *Songs of Experience,* justifies the existence of poor orphans as morally beneficial to the rest of us, for

> Pity would be no more,
> If we did not make somebody Poor[.]

The speaker, we might say, is innocent in a pejorative sense: he is morally obtuse. Blake in fact had first assigned 'Holy Thursday' to a named character, Obtuse Angle, in his manuscript farce, *An Island in the Moon.* It is not fair to incorporate what we know of Obtuse Angle, who seems to be a mathematician, into the very different context of the *Songs of Innocence,* but the poem's earlier placing reminds us that all the *Songs* are dramatic monologues spoken by an implicit character and not by Blake himself. Blake is the ventriloquist, the stage manager, the organizing genius, who presents us with the many voices of the state of innocence.

2. Songs of Experience

Between 1789 and 1793 Blake wrote and engraved a series of poems that in some sense 'answer' the *Songs of Innocence,* and thereafter he nearly always bound the two series together. As he put it in the subtitle to the double volume, the two sets of poems show 'the Two Contrary States of the Human Soul'. We may be tempted by our common-sense notions of maturity and wisdom to take the state of experience as higher than that of innocence, but that is not Blake's view. Some of the speakers of the poems of *Experience* see more widely and deeply than any in *Innocence*, and they do not sound the least bit childlike, but it does not follow that they are themselves in the state of experience, and it is the burden of some of these poems that those who are in that state should 'return' to their original state of innocence. Whether we ought to give the same name to the state thus returned to as we give to the state lost, or whether we should posit a 'higher innocence', has been much debated. It might seem, to one who takes life seriously, that innocence is something we must inevitably lose as we encounter suffering, oppression and death, and that, if we don't despair or 'sell out', we might find enough love and comfort to regain something, at least fleetingly, of the happiness of childhood. We may find it again through children. For Blake, however, experience is a fallen state. It is the 'lapsed Soul' that is addressed in the 'Introduction' to *Experience*, and the title page shows Adam and Eve, figleaved, in agony and surrounded by flames. It is in no way higher than innocence, and it is not clear if it is even a necessary phase or passage, a 'fortunate fall' that enlarges us somehow until we see 'that much more good thereof shall spring', as Milton's Adam states. Good may not spring from it, and it may be possible to avoid it altogether, though there are dangers in trying to prolong innocence by avoiding tests of it, as we shall see. What is crucial to Blake's purposes, without which there would be no point in writing the poems, is that no matter how bleak, hopeless and final the state of experience may seem while you are in it, you may still pass through it. 'States Change', Blake later wrote (in *Milton,* plate 32, line 23), and some states are only apparent, such as 'Death / And Hell & the Grave: States that are not, but ah! Seem to be' (lines 28–9).

The soul is a complicated thing, and Blake's poems exhibit many variations in insight, feeling and courage on the part of their speakers.

Several poems originally in *Innocence* must have struck him as transitional to the state of experience, so when he completed the *Experience* series he transferred them. These are 'The Little Girl Lost' and 'The Little Girl Found', the adventures of Lyca among the lions; 'The School Boy', whose complaint may have seemed a little too strident beside the gentle songs of the sweeper and black boy, who had much more to complain of; and 'The Voice of the Ancient Bard', whose harsh and peremptory tone may have seemed better suited to the fallen world. These transfers should prevent us from regarding either state as sealed off from the other. Innocence is primary and self-sufficient, but experience steals in or pounces upon unwary innocence in our unhappy world (indeed too much wariness might sap innocence from within), while experience can either tighten and petrify as we add winters to our life or loosen and thaw as new days dawn.

The Bard

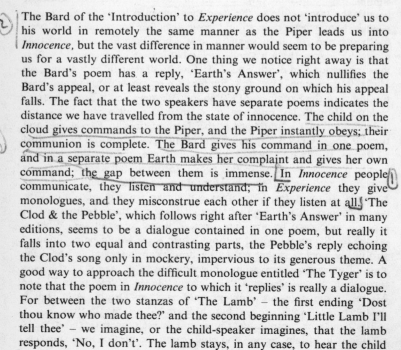

The Bard of the 'Introduction' to *Experience* does not 'introduce' us to his world in remotely the same manner as the Piper leads us into *Innocence,* but the vast difference in manner would seem to be preparing us for a vastly different world. One thing we notice right away is that the Bard's poem has a reply, 'Earth's Answer', which nullifies the Bard's appeal, or at least reveals the stony ground on which his appeal falls. The fact that the two speakers have separate poems indicates the distance we have travelled from the state of innocence. The child on the cloud gives commands to the Piper, and the Piper instantly obeys; their communion is complete. The Bard gives his command in one poem, and in a separate poem Earth makes her complaint and gives her own command; the gap between them is immense. In *Innocence* people communicate, they listen and understand; in *Experience* they give monologues, and they misconstrue each other if they listen at all. 'The Clod & the Pebble', which follows right after 'Earth's Answer' in many editions, seems to be a dialogue contained in one poem, but really it falls into two equal and contrasting parts, the Pebble's reply echoing the Clod's song only in mockery, impervious to its generous theme. A good way to approach the difficult monologue entitled 'The Tyger' is to note that the poem in *Innocence* to which it 'replies' is really a dialogue. For between the two stanzas of 'The Lamb' – the first ending 'Dost thou know who made thee?' and the second beginning 'Little Lamb I'll tell thee' – we imagine, or the child-speaker imagines, that the lamb responds, 'No, I don't'. The lamb stays, in any case, to hear the child answer his own question, meeting his eyes in expectation. The 'Tyger', however, says nothing, and remains sublimely aloof from the speaker's troubled questions, which redound upon his head as the poem seals itself off by repeating its opening stanza. The characters in 'London', finally, fail even to make statements but are reduced to mere cries, sighs and curses. Indeed, most of the speakers and characters of the *Songs of Experience* have erected what Blake later called 'Selfhoods' in order to shut out the painful world.

The Bard's introduction is difficult in a manner characteristic of much of Blake's poetry written from this time onwards: it is dense and telegraphic, cosmic in its range and thick with biblical and Miltonic phrases. None the less its general purport comes through on a first reading: the Bard, like a biblical prophet, calls on the world to leave its darkness and return ('convert' in the original sense) to its former state of light. Much of the power and fascination of the poem, like those of 'The Tyger' and many others, lies in just this combination of urgent simplicity and cryptic symbolism and allusion. Something very important seems to be taking place, half visible through a veil, and we rouse our faculties to try to lift it.

> Hear the voice of the Bard!
> Who Present, Past, & Future sees
> Whose ears have heard,
> The Holy Word,
> That walk'd among the ancient trees.
>
> Calling the lapsed Soul
> And weeping in the evening dew:
> That might controll,
> The starry pole;
> And fallen fallen light renew!

The first problem is with the syntax, assuming that by now the reader has learned to ignore Blake's strange punctuation. Are 'Calling' and 'weeping' governed by 'The Holy Word', the nearest plausible subject, or do we go all the way back to 'the voice of the Bard'? And is 'That might control ... And ... renew' parallel to 'That walk'd', and thus governed by 'The Holy Word' as well, or is its subject 'the lapsed Soul'? It may not be possible to sort out the syntax if we are still in the dark about what the Bard's ears have heard. Though 'ancient trees' seems a novel way to describe the Garden of Eden, the Bard must be referring to God's visit on the evening after the Fall: 'And they heard the voice of the Lord God walking in the garden in the cool of the day: and

Adam and his wife hid themselves from the presence of the Lord God amongst the trees of the garden' (Genesis 3:8). The voice of God becomes the Holy Word probably by way of Milton's version of this scene in *Paradise Lost,* where it is the Son, the Word, and not the Father, who comes to the Garden to judge Adam and Eve. Nothing is said there or in Genesis about weeping, though Milton calls the Son 'the mild Judge', yet the Bard, who sees all of time at once, reminds us of the Man of Sorrows who wept over Lazarus before raising him from the dead. Here Jesus seems to sympathize with the fall of nature, for he weeps 'in' the evening dew, just as the dew and the setting sun are emblems of the Fall of Man. (Milton – Book X, line 92 – has 'the Sun in Western cadence low', 'cadence' deriving from the Latin *cadere,* 'to fall', as in Blake's 'fallen fallen light'. And in *Jerusalem* – plate 42, lines 6–8 – Blake writes, 'the Divine Saviour descended / . . . the Divine Vision wept / Like evening dew'.)

It is best to take 'The Holy Word', then, as calling to 'the lapsed Soul', as the Lord called unto the lapsed Adam in the garden, though since the Bard will immediately turn to call the fallen earth, it may not matter much which subject we assign. Indeed, by having heard the Word himself – by having ears *and* hearing – the Bard's voice repeats the Holy Word to us; he becomes one with it. As for who might control the starry pole, God or Christ already rules heaven, according to orthodox tradition, but the point of the 'calling' is that the fallen Soul itself 'might' rise above the starry heights if it can return or awaken from its night of slumber. 'Pole' meant the sky or heaven as a whole, not any particular part such as the north pole or the zenith, and Milton also uses 'starry pole' in this sense in *Paradise Lost.* To control the starry sky and to renew fallen light are parallel in phrasing and probably similar in meaning. If so, this lends the impression that the lapsed Soul is a fallen star, but the image evoked may be more that of the setting sun, which allows the stars, mere specks of light, to appear only in its absence. The sun, as the principle of light itself, 'controls' the stars not only in commanding them but perhaps in an older sense of overmastering them. The 'risen' Soul is thus expected to shine with such a light that the stars are eclipsed.

Yet it is not a star or the sun that the Bard addresses; it is the earth.

> O Earth O Earth return!
> Arise from out the dewy grass;
> Night is worn,

> And the morn
> Rises from the slumberous mass.

> Turn away no more:
> Why wilt thou turn away
> The starry floor
> The watry shore
> Is giv'n thee till the break of day.

The Bard is taking the stance Jeremiah took as he addressed the unreceptive souls of Israel: 'O earth earth earth, hear the word of the Lord' (Jeremiah 22:29). This metaphor is brought to life in Isaiah and the Gospels where the people are likened to different kinds of ground and the Word of God to seed; Earth in her answer seems to want the sower to sow her, and the 'plowman' to 'plow' her, but despairs of their happening at night. The Bard insists that it is dawn, and calls on the earth to rise as the sun rises. In this starry poem, however, the earth also acquires an astronomical connotation – the planet turning on its axis. This image breeds further complexities that may be impossible to sort out. Is the Bard asking the earth to stop rotating, or to rotate backwards? If it were to keep on rotating, after all, dawn would arrive on schedule. And in what sense can the earth be said to rise? Milton's Raphael tells Adam not to worry unduly

> Whether the Sun predominant in Heav'n
> Rise on the Earth, or Earth rise on the Sun,
> Hee from the East his flaming road begin,
> Or Shee from the West her silent course advance
> With inoffensive pace that spinning sleeps
> On her soft Axle,
> (*Paradise Lost*, Book VIII, lines 160–64)

and perhaps we should take his advice, though this very passage may have provided Blake with his rising earth and 'slumberous mass'. What Blake gives us is a set of mixed metaphors, but the metaphors have subterranean connections among themselves and they are brilliantly mixed.

The ending has a quiet power.

> The starry floor
> The watry shore
> Is giv'n thee till the break of day.

If the starry pole is really a floor, then the place where Earth should rise and walk is above the stars, where the sun shines and the Holy

Word reigns. If Earth sees the stars from beneath, she is fallen or upside down or both. The watery shore is land's end, or the earth's limit, and so in a way is the starry floor; they are given to Earth by providence to sustain her until morning. In *Jerusalem* Blake writes of 'the Limit of Contraction', which is established by an act of mercy to prevent humankind from falling into complete nothingness. On the other hand, these two limits are also the verges of dreadful chaos, and Earth finds no comfort in them. We may take the last line, then, as also saying that the starry floor and watery shore are given to Earth *only* until daybreak.

The Bard's speech assumes that the fallen Soul or sleeping Earth can rise of her own will. But Earth manages only to raise up her head, which is too filled with dread and despair to imagine she can do anything unaided. The 'Stony dread' she feels echoes the 'stony ground' of the parable of the sower, and she cannot take in the Word of the Bard. Instead she feels 'Prison'd' and kept in a den by 'Starry Jealousy' and she mistakes the Bard for someone very different: 'I hear the Father of the ancient men / Selfish father of men'. This father is presumably 'Starry Jealousy', who sounds like the jealous God of the Old Testament seen as a god of night, as well as a harsh father who represses the healthy desires of his virgin daughter. Seeing herself as victimized by another, she can only conceive of being liberated by another, and so she concludes by calling on the Father (the voice she takes to be the Father) to

> Break this heavy chain,
> That does freeze my bones around[.]

What we have in the end is a stalemate between the Bard who commands Earth to arise and Earth who commands the Bard-as-father to set her free.

Earth has her defenders among Blake scholars. She is right, it is argued, to hear the voice of 'Starry Jealousy' in the voice of the Bard, for she remembers the first evening in the Garden of Eden better than the Bard does. In the Bard's version it is the Holy Word who comes, and he only calls and weeps, but in Earth's version, which is the book of Genesis, it is God the Father who comes, not to weep but to punish Adam and Eve by banishing them from the Garden. They have lost the 'delight' of 'free Love' that was theirs before they transgressed an arbitrary rule. The trouble with this reading, of course, is that it takes Genesis as gospel, as it were, and yet there is no reason why we should. Blake certainly did not. He wrote his own version of Genesis, *The Book of Urizen,* in which he makes clear that it is the disarray of the human faculties that causes the fall of the human race and not an external agent like God or the serpent.

> No more could they rise at will
> In the infinite void, but bound down
> To earth by their narrowing perceptions[.]

(Chap: IX, lines 45–7)

Some readers hear a repellent peremptoriness and smug self-certainty in the Bard, whose sole source of authority is his own claim to be inspired. No doubt if we met someone in 'real life' who spoke like the Bard we would rightly suspect him of imposture, but there seems to be nothing in the poem, or in the other Bard poems, to trigger this suspicion. Blake made the same claim for himself in several later poems and in letters to friends, and indeed the tone of the narrators of his longer works can only be called 'bardic'. We may have doubts about Blake's own visions and their authority, but we must not take our doubts about Blake to be Blake's doubts about the Bard. It would be more in the spirit of the two poems to allow that we who find the Bard grating may be lapsed souls ourselves. No doubt we would rather be piped to, but we are no longer innocent, and the voice suited to our stony ears is a bit louder than we will someday require. At least we should grant that the Bard, whatever his limits, sees more broadly and deeply than many of the speakers of the *Songs of Experience,* who are examples of the Selfhoods generated by narrow perceptions and anxious fears.

This is not to say that Blake believed that all human woes are self-induced. The Chimney Sweeper and Little Black Boy do not afflict themselves. But, as states, innocence and experience are subject to our own energies and intentions. Innocence is not immunity to suffering but a faith in life and an openness to others that mitigate that suffering by placing it in a larger universe. Experience is marked by despair and a withdrawal into one's private self. Ultimately we can see that the nettlesome bards 'belong' to the thorny ground of fallen Earth, but that is not to reduce them to the same level of delusion. The bards are one means of universal redemption, not least because they call us to action against the social evils that make innocent people suffer.

Contrary States

One of the pleasures of the *Songs of Innocence and of Experience* is to compare the matched or contrary poems. 'The Tyger' matches 'The

25

Lamb', as we have seen, 'The Human Abstract' answers 'The Divine Image', and 'Infant Sorrow' replies to 'Infant Joy', while there are two Nurse's Songs, two Chimney Sweeper poems, and two entitled 'Holy Thursday'. Moreover, perhaps 'London' is a kind of contrary of 'The Ecchoing Green'. Before we turn to some of these pairs of poems, however, it will be worth looking again at 'The Clod & the Pebble', which is a pair of contraries contained in one poem.

> Love seeketh not Itself to please,
> Nor for itself hath any care;
> But for another gives its ease,
> And builds a Heaven in Hells despair.

> So sang a little Clod of Clay,
> Trodden with the cattles feet:
> But a Pebble of the brook,
> Warbled out these metres meet.

> Love seeketh only Self to please,
> To bind another to its delight;
> Joys in anothers loss of ease,
> And builds a Hell in Heavens despite.

The subject of this little debate is so central to Blake's view of things and so simply and candidly worded that I am tempted to say that Blake sets it before us as a test of our ability to read him right. But how do we read it? The song of the Clod describes self-sacrificing Christian love and its redemptive effects in uncompromising terms. We may find it impossibly heroic but we can hardly withhold our praise for it – until we come to the end of the Clod's half of the poem: 'Trodden with the cattles feet'. That gives us pause. Is that the consequence of such noble self-denial? It is such a lowly, undignified martyrdom and almost comically anticlimactic in its placing, like a philosopher in a farce who intones lofty thoughts as he pitches down the cellar stairs.

The Pebble, though we cannot at first endorse its self-centredness, is not only given the last word but suffers no indignity. It will continue to warble contentedly about its joys and delights, impervious to the flowing stream or any creature's feet. With these considerations in mind, some readers have found the Pebble healthy in its self-assertiveness and the Clod extreme and one-sided in its altruism; the Clod's virtue seems abstract and not much like the interactive individualism of the children who play together in the *Songs of Innocence*. One critic has compared the Clod, who 'builds a Heaven in Hells despair', to the God, priest and king of the second 'Chimney Sweeper' poem, 'Who make up a heaven of our misery'; the Clod thus becomes a repressive figure, offering only illusory compensation for the miseries of this world. Balancing the pluses and minuses, then, we might conclude that there is no conclusion and call it a stalemate.

Like some of the parables of Jesus, this poem divides its readers into sheep and goats, or rather clods and pebbles. I think the pro-Pebble party has projected its own discomfort over the Clod's message on to the narrator or Blake, and reduced the poem to moral incoherence rather than face up to what the Clod has to say. Similarly, many who heard Jesus had minds too stony or pebbly to be impressed by his claim that the Kingdom was among them, but a few impressionable clods in his audience, fools that became wise (in St Paul's words), took the news to heart and began building heavens in the midst of despair. Should we be amused that the Clod is trodden with the cattle's feet? That is more or less what happened to Jesus himself, and all the martyrs of the Church; the Crucifixion was an undignified death, and Stephen the first martyr was stoned with impervious stones. To place the Pebble's song second is not to give it 'the last word' any more than Earth by speaking second refutes the Bard, or experience as a whole refutes innocence. Indeed, the Crucifixion did not refute the teachings of Jesus, for Easter was his reply, and we have not yet heard his Last Word.

Does his concern lead to dream heaven ??

In my view, a better comparison than the God, priest and king of the second 'Chimney Sweeper' poem is the first Chimney Sweeper himself, whose warm concern for Tom Dacre leads to Tom's little dream-heaven in the midst of the hellish life of hot, dark chimneys. We may call this an illusion, but it is not imposed on the miserable for the benefit of the rich and powerful. The Clod's song, moreover, can be taken in a much more this-worldly sense than Tom's dream easily allows: 'Hells despair', where love builds heaven, sounds much more like a state many people inhabit in this life than a literal hell like Dante's or Milton's, which are closed off from the interventions of love. At the time Blake was working on the *Songs of Experience* he also wrote, 'The most sublime act is to set another before you' (E 36), and in his longer poems he constantly insists that we annihilate our Selfhoods. In *Thel* there is another 'Clod of Clay' who says 'we live not for ourselves' and goes on to describe the mysteries of divine love and redemption. We may disbelieve the mysteries and retreat from them as Thel does, but we must not conclude that Blake agrees with us or that 'The Clod and the Pebble' is a subtle exercise in irony. Be clods, he is saying. Be simple, impressionable readers. Be simple, impressionable lovers of your fellow human beings, too, and ye shall inherit the Kingdom.

The 'Holy Thursday' of *Experience* sounds like so direct a reply to its counterpart in *Innocence* that it is not hard to picture a second adult observer of the orphans taking the first observer by the lapels and giving him a good shake. 'Is this a holy thing to see', just because it is Holy Thursday and they are all in church? 'Is that trembling cry a song? / Can it be a song of joy?' You are deluding yourself, sir, if you think they are all well cared for by those you are pleased to call wise guardians of the poor. This second adult does get the last word, but less because he speaks second than because the kind of 'innocence' we sensed in the first speaker had something stale, pious and smug about it, and the 'experience' of the second speaker has not driven him inward in despair but prompted him to speak out, like a prophet or bard, on behalf of others. His poem may not be as subtle or interesting as his slow friend's, since the reader has no need to sift out acute perceptions from obtuse conceptions; he means what he says and knows what he means. He does pass rather quickly between two 'lands', one that is 'rich and fruitful' and one that is a 'land of poverty', one where it is eternal winter and one where the sun shines and rain falls. They are the same land, of course, but they seem utterly different to the two peoples who inhabit them, those who have been 'reduced to misery' and those who have, perhaps unfairly because of 'usurous' practices, escaped it. Disraeli in *Sybil* was to write of 'the two Nations' of England and William Booth was to entitle a book *In Darkest England,* as if it were Africa. In the 1960s Michael Harrington's *The Other America* revived the metaphor on both sides of the Atlantic.

Blake ends his poem with a Utopian vision of the redeemed land.

> For where-e'er the sun does shine,
> And where-e'er the rain does fall:
> Babe can never hunger there,
> Nor poverty the mind appall.

This last line seems to have several meanings, or several applications, depending on how one takes 'appall', a word that Blake must have liked for its varying resonances, for he uses it in several other poems. The usual modern sense derives from its passive form – 'He was appalled by the poverty he saw' – and means 'shock' or 'make indignant'. That sense would apply to the speaker of the poem, and to us, its readers. Its root sense, however, to 'make pale', is summoned by its active form, as we have it here. If we think of the pallor as caused by fear and guilt (the sense 'appall' probably has in 'London'), it might apply to the speaker of 'Holy Thursday' in *Innocence,* whose conventional pieties look like a defence against his own complicity in the institutionalized suffering of the children. We might take the 'mind' that poverty appalls, finally, not as an observer's at all, but as a poor person's, a mind weakened and drained by misery until it is as tremulous as the feeble song of the children, or as dry and hardened as the youthful harlot's mind whose curse concludes 'London'. Whatever mind we imagine as appalled, it is important that we see that it is with 'mind' that Blake ends his poem. Innocence is a state of mind, and its preservation is vital not only to the growth and happiness of individuals but to the reformation of an 'appalling' society.

The second 'Chimney Sweeper' poem has two speakers, an adult who introduces the poem in three lines, and a chimney sweeper who tells his brief story in the remaining nine. The sweeper seems older than his fellows in *Innocence* though he looks no older in the design; he certainly has a much clearer understanding of the adult world and its dishonesties. But the adult speaker has seemed to some readers as 'appalled' into obtuseness.

> A little black thing among the snow:
> Crying weep, weep. in notes of woe!
> Where are thy father & mother? say?

To describe a child as a 'thing' is to betray a failure of empathy, they say, and the echo of 'poor little thing' suggests the condescending pity that we sensed in the observer at St Paul's. The speaker seems to be exhibiting the child as a case in point. But though we may feel uneasy about the tone, the case is the same with the Chimney Sweeper and Black Boy of *Innocence.* They are no less exhibits; they simply say their poems without a framing narrator. And if we try to make something out of the tone of the narrator, our attention is deflected from what is obviously the main interest of the poem, the speech of the boy.

> They are both gone up to the church to pray.
>
> Because I was happy upon the heath.
> And smil'd among the winters snow:
> They clothed me in the clothes of death.
> And taught me to sing the notes of woe.
>
> And because I am happy. & dance and sing.
> They think they have done me no injury:
> And are gone to praise God & his Priest & King
> Who make up a heaven of our misery.

29

This is one of the bluntest condemnations of hypocrisy in all the *Songs*. The father and mother who should be caring for their child have made him a chimney sweeper – though the fact that he knows where they are at the moment makes it unclear whether they have sold him to a master sweeper or put him to work themselves – and they have gone to church to praise God. For what? For making a heaven to compensate for the misery of this life? That is not how the boy sees it, for it is not only God they praise but also the authorities of this world, who 'make up a heaven', somehow, 'of our misery'.

Some readers have been disturbed by the boy's tone as well. His syntax seems a little too formal, and he endues his speech with somewhat overdone epithets, such as 'clothes of death' and 'notes of woe' (though the latter may be an echo of the questioner's phrase), as if he is seeing himself as an exhibit and is reciting well-rehearsed lines. He seems too knowing in his critique of religion. Although he says that he dances and sings, we do not enter into his innocence the way we do that of Tom Dacre's friend. Again, though, if we dwell on these artificialities and improbabilities, we may miss the important points. He is not, after all, a real child, and if Blake failed to make him seem real to us, it may be because he has turned the poem to different ends.

It seems to me that the most 'appalling' word in this poem is 'because'. We wonder if the boy fully understands just how diabolically contrary his father and mother sound when he says it is *because* he was happy that they put him in black clothes and made him cry 'weep'. He may use 'because' the way the sweeper in *Innocence* sometimes uses 'so', indicating sequence but connoting consequence. To him the succession of states, from singing happy songs of innocence, even on a wintry heath, to singing the woeful songs his parents taught him, must seem linked causally; to us other motives suggest themselves, misguided and cruel but less perverse. Yet things are revealed to babes that the wise and prudent are blind to, and it may be true that it was the very happiness of the boy that prompted his parents to injure him. The 'Nurses Song' in *Experience* portrays the same perversity.

> When the voices of children, are heard on the green
> And whisperings are in the dale:
> The days of my youth rise fresh in my mind,
> My face turns green and pale.

Envy and resentment taint her mind – she may even suspect the whisperings are about her (and, being the person she is, she may be right) – and her response is to put an end to the happiness that stirs them by calling the children home. (By contrast, the Nurse in *Innocence*, whose 'heart is at rest', is easily persuaded to let the children stay out later.) Blake understood well how it is that some people hate innocence and want to destroy it, usually because they cannot bear the memory of their own lost 'days of my youth' and want to repress it. Usually, too, they make their hatred acceptable to themselves by disguising it as love, but children see through it. So Ona, the maiden who forgot her fear and made love with a youth, becomes 'A Little Girl Lost' when she goes to her father, apparently in the hope that he will bless her love.

> To her father white
> Came the maiden bright:
> But his loving look,
> Like the holy book,
> All her tender limbs with terror shook.

Had Freud known Blake, the 'Ona Complex' might be as familiar as his Greek terms, Eros, Thanatos and the Oedipus Complex: this 'loving look' contains the seeds of a whole psychological theory. It is like the 'dark secret love' of the canker worm that destroys the 'crimson joy' of the 'Sick Rose'; he flies in the night, whereas Ona and her lover 'Naked in the sunny beams delight'.

The haters of innocence may also disguise their hatred as duty or care – 'the Priestly care' that all admire in 'A Little Boy Lost' or the probable self-satisfaction in the Nurse's mind, with which she deceives herself that she has acted out of duty rather than envy. Perhaps the paradigm for this disguise is Satan's speech to himself as he first comes upon Adam and Eve in *Paradise Lost*: 'And should I at your harmless innocence / Melt, as I do', it is, however, 'public reason just' that compels him to 'deliver [them] to woe' (Book IV, lines 388–9, 368). Satan, however, not being a Christian hypocrite, is honest enough to avow that he is moved by honour, empire and revenge. By contrast, the father and mother of the chimney sweeper are no doubt too swathed in the conceits of virtue to recognize the desire for revenge that moves them to afflict the nearest reminder of their own lost innocence.

The second 'because' is less startling – 'And because I am happy. & dance & sing. / They think they have done me no injury' – but we may be surprised to hear that the boy is still happy. The earlier chimney sweepers have taught us that even under terrible conditions children can be resourceful and imaginative, filling the little nooks and crannies of their lives with warmth and colour. In a poem written in a copy of

31

Blake's earliest book, *Poetical Sketches* (Penguin edition, page 62), an old shepherd sings,

> Innocence is a Winter's gown;
> So clad, we'll abide life's pelting storm
> That makes our limbs quake, if our hearts be warm.

The Chimney Sweeper still wears his innocence under his black uniform, but perhaps it is becoming soiled by it. His innocence seems to be giving way to experience; there is a difference, at least, between him and the sweepers who seem not to realize that they have been injured. Are we to see him as embarked on experience's wintry seas and destined to drown in spirit like the envious nurses and fathers, though they keep their selfhoods afloat on impervious little rafts? Though we may worry about his precocious insights into his parents' hypocrisy and the social function of religion, these insights are of the sort that turns people not into priests and modest dames with birches but into bards and prophets. There is a touch of prophetic vision in his final lines about the God, priest and king 'Who make up a heaven of our misery'. Whether the boy fully knows what he says we may not be able to decide, for the lines can be read in several ways, some of them sounding much like Marx and Feuerbach, who saw the enrichment of heaven as a projection of the impoverishment of earth. But he has grasped the truth about the Church (and State) as clearly as he has understood his father and mother.

'The Human Abstract'

Perhaps the most pointed set of contraries, certainly the most explicit in its teaching, is 'The Divine Image' (*Innocence*) and 'The Human Abstract' (*Experience*). But many readers have found the point blunted by their impression that 'The Divine Image' is too abstract, that nothing like an image can be seen in it. The poem claims that the four abstract virtues are human.

> For Mercy has a human heart
> Pity, a human face:
> And Love, the human form divine,
> And Peace, the human dress.

Yet the picture that emerges seems not so much human as what one critic has called 'a monster of abstractions'. It may be that the poem verges on what has been called a 'performative self-contradiction', the sort of thing Epimenides the Cretan achieved when he called all Cretans liars, but it breeds monsters only if we lack a human heart and fail to enter into its spirit. The point of the song, after all, is that these virtues to whom everyone prays as if to a transcendent God, abstracted from our daily life, are really here among us, human as much as divine, indeed divine in so far as they are truly human; if we practise these virtues, God dwells in our midst. It is as if Blake starts where thousands of prayers begin, in abstractions – 'Have mercy upon us'; 'Grant us thy peace'; 'O Father of mercies and God of all comfort, our only help in time of need' – and gently, through a kind of liturgy (the poem is found in hymnals today), leads the one who prays back to all the others who are in distress and likewise praying. The recognition of kinship with 'heathen, turk or jew', who are really praying to the same God, is a kind of answer to the prayer. It is as great a shift as this poem could well make, and it manages quietly to make the crucial break with the other-worldly projections that priests impose on the innocent. We may prefer poems with more concrete imagery, but this poem is no more abstract than it has to be, unless we are to rule out such religious subjects as the Incarnation, which Blake brilliantly evokes, in fact, in his little abstract phrase, 'the human form divine'.

Blake's first attempt at a contrary to 'The Divine Image', which he entitled 'A Divine Image' (E 32), posits four opposing vices – cruelty, jealousy, terror and secrecy – and constructs something like Moloch, a 'fiery Forge' or furnace with a 'hungry Gorge', certainly a divine image of a sort. This poem was included in one known copy of the joint *Songs,* but it was replaced in all the other copies by a much more interesting poem. Blake tried the title 'The Human Image' in his notebook draft, and then hit upon 'The Human Abstract' as a fuller contrary. 'Abstract' will become a key term throughout Blake's works, and he will exploit all its connotations.

The speaker of 'The Human Abstract' systematically redefines the four virtues of 'The Divine Image', changing the sequence of the first two in order to put the most striking revision first.

> Pity would be no more,
> If we did not make somebody Poor:
> And Mercy no more could be,
> If all were as happy as we;
>
> And mutual fear brings peace;
> Till the selfish loves increase.

> Then Cruelty knits a snare,
> And spreads his baits with care.

This speaker seems almost innocent in his cynicism, so candid are his rationalizations; Blake is exhibiting what many supposed Christians, and especially the priests, really believe but dare not say or even admit to themselves. We may even be tempted briefly to take the speaker as a kind of Nietzschean critic of Christianity, unmasking the base hidden motives beneath the noble rhetoric. Certainly many would agree that pity is not the same as compassion or solidarity. Hannah Arendt in *On Revolution* has written that pity 'has a vested interest in the existence of the unhappy'. Blake's speaker, however, really does cling to pity, along with mercy and peace, as essential to his mental universe. Like the observer of the innocent 'Holy Thursday' he cherishes pity itself rather than those for whom he feels it. He can bask in delicious sentimentality while sounding objective and worldly at the same time – indeed his theory of peace as a cold war is the foundation of the modern world order.

After line 5 the tone seems to change. Pretence is dropped. The kind of love that interests the speaker turns out to be selfish and plural – plural, because if love is selfish, there cannot be a single binding love among a multitude of selves. But the love of 'The Divine Image' gives way in the fourth couplet to a new character altogether, 'Cruelty', who becomes the chief actor in the rest of the poem, an allegory about the tree of mystery or religion. We are shown the origin and true character of the Church, which draws the innocents into its clutches, manacles their minds and, as Blake put it in 'The Garden of Love', binds with briars their joys and desires.

The snare and baits made by Cruelty, since they are not part of the horticultural imagery that follows, we may take as a variant of the tree-growing, which culminates in an attractive fruit to snare the unwary; the next three stanzas, in other words, describe in different metaphors and greater detail how Cruelty does his 'knitting'.

> He sits down with holy fears,
> And waters the ground with tears:
> Then Humility takes its root
> Underneath his foot.
>
> Soon spreads the dismal shade
> Of Mystery over his head;
> And the Catterpillar and Fly,
> Feed on the Mystery.

> And it bears the fruit of Deceit,
> Ruddy and sweet to eat;
> And the Raven his nest has made
> In its thickest shade.

The word 'holy' is seldom favourable in Blake's usage. The speaker of the second 'Holy Thursday' echoes the title sarcastically as he begins, 'Is this a holy thing to see[?]. In the 'Age of Gold' portrayed at the beginning of 'A Little Girl Lost' the youth and maiden are naked 'To the holy light', but at the end, with the introduction of the maiden's father, the only thing that is holy is 'the holy book', a simile for the terrifying 'love' that threatens to blight her life. The priest in 'A Little Boy Lost', trembling with rage at the boy's free thinking, defends 'our most holy Mystery' by burning him in 'a holy place'. Holiness and mystery are the same thing: they are an 'abstraction' or 'withdrawal' of living spiritual wealth from the human community, locked up and doled out by self-appointed guardians who deceive the community into believing that this confiscated wealth comes from above and is graciously granted to those who are properly abject. Blake believed that Jesus came to do away with this false impropriation and to redistribute the wealth. As Jesus died he rent the veil of the temple and became the final high priest; he entered the Holy of Holies and passed out its manna to everyone. Blake brought to a climax two of his works written at this time (*The Marriage of Heaven and Hell* and *Visions of the Daughters of Albion* – see final plates) by repristinating the word 'holy' in the spirit of Jesus's radical demystification: 'For every thing that lives is Holy'.

'Humility' fares no better in Blake's book. 'God wants not Man to Humble himself', he writes in *The Everlasting Gospel*:

> Thou art a Man God is no more
> Thy own humanity learn to adore.

(Penguin edition, page 859, lines 65, 75–6)

The humility that takes root here might be the false humility of the 'servants of God', as priests style themselves, but since it grows under Cruelty's foot we might rather take it as the humility required of the faithful if they are to be admitted to the 'Mystery'. Holy fears, then, the reverence proper before the holy altar, condense into holy water in the form of Cruelty's false tears (or are they the real tears of suffering innocents?), sprinkled on the ground to prepare it for sowing. But there is no seed, perhaps because Blake did not want to evoke the

35

idea of the seed as Word, as in Jesus's parable of the sower. If the ground (as in the parable) represents the minds of the faithful, then holy water alone is enough to engender humility, for they are prepared by holy fears to grovel. In this imagery, in fact, Blake seems to revive the etymology of 'humility' (from *humus*, 'earth').

It is hard to contemplate the allegorical tree of this poem without thinking of the Tree of Knowledge in the Garden of Eden. (A kindred species may be found in 'A Poison Tree'.) Cruelty's tree produces a ruddy fruit, the taste of which will surely cause the death of one's spirit and happiness, as the raven, the bird of death, proclaims. But this tree is also the Church, for when it grows leaves they become the shade of Mystery. 'Mystery' means not only something 'holy': it is a theological term, the Greek for 'sacrament', and according to Blake those who administer the sacraments 'feed' on them like caterpillars and flies, parasites at another's feast. 'As the caterpiller chooses the fairest leaves to lay her eggs on,' Blake wrote, 'so the priest lays his curse on the fairest joys' (E 37). In calling it a 'shade' Blake is reviving the etymology of 'Mystery', too, for it derives from a root word meaning 'to close the eyes'. The humble parishioner blindly gives everything to the Church and then gratefully accepts a nibble or sip as a mysterious gift. The mystery of it all is metaphorically 'over his head', as the 'dismal shade' blocks the light (of understanding) from his brain.

When the black bird of death makes its nest in the tree's 'thickest shade' we may be reminded of Jesus's parable of the mustard seed, which grows into a tree of great size 'so that all the fowls of the air may lodge under the shadow of it' (Mark 4:32). That is the tree of the Kingdom of God, later taken to mean the Church; Blake's abstract tree is a satanic parody of it.

The final stanza brings the story to an end with a dramatic flourish.

> The Gods of the earth and sea,
> Sought thro' Nature to find this Tree
> But their search was all in vain:
> There grows one in the Human Brain[.]

It tells us little, however, that we did not already know. We knew the tree is a product of the human brain as it is an allegory, a creature of human vices such as cruelty and humility or the poverty that we 'make' (line 2). It is thus a little beside the point for deities to search 'thro' Nature' for the tree. In Blake's universe, as it unfolds in the longer works written from the 1790s onwards, 'Nature' is almost always a barrier to spiritual insight and energy, and nature's agents or regents are only secondary falsehoods compounded of the original error of taking nature as something external and independent of our minds. It is also a little puzzling that he should end the poem with 'Brain' rather than 'Soul' or 'Mind' (the rhyme word 'vain' in the preceding line is hardly indispensable), for the brain is the material or 'natural' aspect of the mind, and the gods of nature might be expected to look there early in their search for the tree.

It may be that Blake tried a more subtle manoeuvre, like the shifts of perspective so frequent in his later works, where 'we become what we behold' and confirm our own narrow beliefs by shrinking ourselves until we fit them. For 'Humility' is not only the root of the tree but its fruit: if you eat it you will be deceived into thinking yourself a humble and unworthy worm. If you think of yourself as a natural creature, rather than a spiritual creator, your mind will indeed become just a brain, and a 'roof shaggy wild' will enclose 'in an orb, [your] fountain of thought', as Blake put it in a later poem (*The Book of Urizen*, plate 10, lines 33–4). 'Brainy' people such as Isaac Newton and John Locke reduced us all to walking brains, blank slates tied by gravity to our necks, while spiritual people such as the prophets and the bards tried to awaken us from our earthly delusions so we would rise like the sun. The Church, though it claims to be supernatural, and proves it every Sunday by changing wine into blood, has made peace with nature, especially human nature, and dedicated its best brains to getting material wealth. Perhaps unfairly, given his usual disparagement of nature, Blake, like a good Enlightenment sceptic, hearkens back to the classical gods of nature and pictures them baffled by this upstart Christian tree. Since they can find the tree nowhere in nature, the tree must be, by implication, 'unnatural'. An orthodox Christian apologist would reply that that is just the point – the Church transcends nature – but before the apologist can point to the Church's heavenly origin, Blake points to its true origin in a more mundane place, the human brain.

The design suggests that it is out of Cruelty's brain that the original snare is created. Pictured as a bearded old man on his knees, a figure whom Blake will later name Urizen, Cruelty seems to be trying to extricate himself from a rope that lies across his head, but he might also be braiding the rope out of his hair. There is a parallel rope on one side, with cross strands in some copies, making a net. It is hard to resist the impression that he is caught in his own snare. A large tree stands near him, quite firmly rooted in the ground, but we can easily imagine

37

the ropes, which seem attached to the ground on both sides of the old man, as taking root and coming up near by as trees of mystery. He looks less cruel than sorrowful or fearful. In *The Book of Urizen* the final phase of the Fall of Man from a primal exuberant innocence is brought about by a 'woven hipocrisy' that grows out of Urizen's 'sorrowing soul'.

> None could break the Web, no wings of fire . . .
> So twisted the cords, & so knotted
> The meshes: twisted like to the human brain . . .
> And all calld it, The Net of Religion[.]

(plate 25, lines 19–22)

'The Tyger'

In a short book like this one we must skip more poems than we discuss. Even if there were more space, I think new readers of Blake find it more helpful to follow a few detailed discussions closely than to take in a general survey that comments lightly on all the *Songs*. Blake would have agreed with the dictum that 'God dwells in the details'. He said himself, again and again, that it is in 'Minute Particulars' that art and ideas dwell, and that these 'little ones' are members of the divine body. He also said, in an angry note in the margins of a book on art, that 'To Generalize is to be an Idiot' (E 641), a hard maxim to live up to but excellent advice to one starting out with Blake.

I shall leave to the reader, then, the marvellous tales of little boys and girls who are lost and (sometimes) found, as well as a bouquet of poems about flowers. It is worth noting that, except for 'The Blossom', which is really about birds, all the flower poems are in *Experience,* as if Blake is avoiding the obvious association of flowers with innocent girls. Roses, lilies and sunflowers have distinct meanings in his own floral symbolism, and so do the metaphors of thorn, blight and heliotropism. But we shall turn now to the two most magnificent short poems in Blake's canon, 'The Tyger' and 'London'.

'The Tyger' is Blake's best-known poem, and it always has been. It is one of the few poems printed in normal typography in Blake's lifetime, first appearing in a little book by Benjamin Malkin in 1806. William Wordsworth or his sister Dorothy copied it from Malkin the next year along with three other poems, and Wordsworth praised Blake on several occasions. In 1811 the poem appeared in a German appreciation of Blake by Henry Crabb Robinson. Charles Lamb pronounced it 'glorious', and glorious it has seemed to most readers ever since. There has been little agreement, however, over what it means, or even if it has a meaning at all.

The poem consists entirely of questions, unlike its counterpart poem 'The Lamb', but the questions are so detailed that they seem to offer answers as they unfold. Even the basic opening question – 'What immortal hand or eye, / Could frame thy fearful symmetry?' – implies that it was a god in human form that made the Tyger, and as the questioner imagines more and more concretely the scene of its creation, he reveals more and more of the facets of its creator. The creator is a blacksmith, for example, a worker in fire, like Hephaestus or Vulcan or Blake's major character Los of later poems. Some of the questions, however, offer more than one possibility: to ask

> In what distant deeps or skies
> Burnt the fire of thine eyes!

is to allow that the creator might be evil, like Satan from the deeps, or good, like the God of the skies. (By this point in the *Songs of Experience*, of course, we have been warned that the God of the skies may not be good either.) In general the questions outrace the implicit answers, until the questions in the fifth and most mysterious stanza bring us to a halt. Looking for clues in the sixth stanza only leads us back to the beginning. We seem to circle round the Tyger, building up an image of it at each turn, only to see it evaporate in the mists. If we start over again, as the 'framing' stanzas seem to ask us to do, we may note more details but feel even more baffled, not to say dizzy from so much circling. In the end we may feel that it is the Tyger that is circling us, and that we are up a tree in the forests of the night.

That there is a change of one word between the first and last stanzas from 'Could frame thy fearful symmetry' to 'Dare frame thy fearful symmetry', suggests that the speaker may have gained a step in his comprehension of the creator, passing from doubts about his power to doubts about his goodness. After imagining the 'shoulder' and 'art', or strength and intelligence, of the creator, and then setting him up in a smithy with hammer, furnace and anvil, the speaker seems to grow more concerned with his morality, as the 'tears' and 'smile' of the fifth stanza also imply. But the shift from 'could' to 'dare' may not mark a real development within the poem, since 'dare' also occurs twice in the second stanza and once in the fourth. The question of the creator's power and of his goodness seem intertwined throughout. Indeed, with the mysteriously incomplete syntax of the third stanza – 'And when thy heart began to beat, / What dread hand? & what dread feet?' – we have an impression that the Tyger and its maker are momentarily fused. 'Hand' must refer to the creator, but 'feet' sounds tigerish, and in any case we are left to complete the sentence ourselves. 'Dread', certainly, would suit the fearful Tyger, but in its two unequivocal applications (before 'hand' and 'grasp') it is an attribute of the creator.

Let us look more closely at the fifth stanza, in which so much seems to be at stake.

> When the stars threw down their spears
> And water'd heaven with their tears:
> Did he smile his work to see?
> Did he who made the Lamb make thee?

The 'When' clause tells of strange cosmic events but tells of them as if they must already be familiar to us; they are the setting or background to the main business of the stanza. But what are these events? They suggest a war in heaven, and the best-known story of a war in heaven is Milton's in *Paradise Lost*. Are the stars, then, the rebel angels, now defeated and weeping over their loss? Since that rebellion was the prime act of evil in the world, are we to take it as not only simultaneous with, but equivalent to, the creation of the Tyger? Is the stars' rebellion, as well as their defeat, a 'work' of the creator? This line of questions, though it may take us no closer to the mark than the speaker's questions, does lead us to the heart of the theological question that Milton is concerned with, the Problem of Evil in a universe controlled by an omnipotent God. The Problem of Evil seems very much on the mind of the Tyger's questioner. The parallels are far from exact, however. Milton's rebel angels did not weep at their defeat in heaven and remained obdurate in hell. Satan throws his 'baleful eyes' around his fallen domain (*Paradise Lost*, Book I, line 56) as if he were the Tyger himself, and indeed he is compared to one as he stalks Adam and Eve in the garden (Book IV, lines 403–8).

Another cosmic event to which these lines may allude is the Nativity, the birth of the Lamb. Milton's version, *On the Morning of Christ's Nativity*, a few lines of which Blake invokes in the opening of *Europe: A Prophecy*, dwells on the defeat at the birth of Christ of the warlike pagan gods, the guises assumed by the rebel angels on earth: 'The flocking shadows pale, / Troop to th'infernal jail', as the new Sun rises (lines 232–3). Such a fading out of the once bright devils might be the tenor of the lines in 'The Tyger'. Blake uses the same imagery to describe the power of morning in a notebook poem.

> The war of swords & spears
> Melted by dewy tears
> Exhales on high
> The Sun is freed from fears
> And with soft grateful tears
> Ascends the sky[.]

('Morning', lines 7–12)

Though in 'The Tyger' those who bear spears and those who shed tears are the same, both descriptions well reflect the natural phenomena of dawn. But in Milton's poem the pagan gods are not the stars, which are benevolent and deferential to the new Star.

> The Stars with deep amaze
> Stand fixt in steadfast gaze,
> Bending one way their precious influence

(lines 69–71)

Perhaps, then, Blake's stars, once warlike, have undergone a conversion to pacifism, and are trying to melt by dewy tears the ferocity of the new-born Tyger. Something of this idea may be found in *America: A Prophecy,* where the thirteen Angels of America, the spirits of the colonies, defect from Albion's command, throw down their golden sceptres and descend, in language from *Paradise Lost* again, 'Headlong from out their heav'nly heights' (plate 12, line 5). The line 'The stars threw down their spears' reappears in *The Four Zoas* (page 64, line 27), where the character Luvah has hidden himself in wrath and summoned the stars, which defect and flee 'naked away'.

None of these possible allusions to Milton, and none of the parallel passages in Blake, is decisive for 'The Tyger', and in the end we are simply left with more questions. Having pondered the biblical and Miltonic stories, the poem's questions ought to resonate more amply and interestingly for us, and these resonances lend a kind of sublimity to the beast in view, but the questions remain unanswered and, we begin to suspect, unanswerable. The climactic question in this poem of questions – 'Did he who made the Lamb make thee?' – has indeed been given every conceivable answer. Some readers have said yes, some no and some that it is an unfathomable mystery beyond mortal scrutiny; some have said he made neither, some that he doesn't exist and some that it is a stupid question posed by an 'idiot Questioner', a phrase Blake used later in *Milton*. It is clear that these differences arise not just from differing readings of difficult lines but from fundamental doubts as to where to take one's stand. Are we to empathize with the speaker, as one who is shaken, as Job was, by evidence that the God he has believed in is incomprehensible? He is not obviously 'characterized' or put into a context, like the Pebble or Chimney Sweeper or Nurse, and he seems to know a great deal about heavenly events, almost like a bard or prophet. On the other hand, all he does is ask questions; the questions get him nowhere; and we wonder, if he is in the forests of the night, what he is doing there in the first place. He may be an unreliable speaker. (When Dante lost his way in a dark wood and met a leopard, lion and wolf, it was his own sins that put him there.) This position may gain support from the drawing of the tiger at the bottom of the page, which few readers have found ferocious or mysterious. The tiger doesn't seem to be burning, it doesn't appear to be night-time (the tiger is clearly visible in natural light) and the one tree near by isn't much of a forest. Isn't this, then, what tigers 'really' look like when you are no longer wandering in a forest of error and dawn comes? For 'does not that mild beam blot / The bat, the owl, the glowing tyger, and the king of night' (*Visions of the Daughters of Albion,* plate 8, lines 4–5)? Aren't tigers just friendly cats, as Lyca found in 'The Little Girl Lost'? For, to alter one of the Proverbs of Hell, 'a fool sees not the same [tyger] that a wise man sees' (Penguin edition, page 183).

To lower the credit of the speaker in this way, and to treat the drawing as an ironic comment on the text, diminishes the poem (and drawing) in the minds of some readers, for to do so is to take the very features that have made it the most loved of Blake's works – its incantatory spell, its overwhelming image, its not-quite-fathomable cosmic events – and father them on a dimwit whom we are invited to reject. It becomes a false poem, a siren song, a snare like Cruelty's to trap the innocent and unwary reader. In defence of this position, though, one could cite the recent theory that Milton's *Paradise Lost* is designed to enlist its readers' sympathies at first for the wrong characters or events, such as Adam in his choice to follow Eve, or Satan in his noble perseverance in defeat, all the more effectively later to educate the reader out of these temptations and into a condition of sober self-governance and steady dedication to truth. Perhaps 'The Tyger', with its disappointing tomcat at the bottom, is meant to take us through a similar process. Like Dante, we cannot arrive at heaven without an education in hell.

Some readers have taken a stance even farther from the speaker and interpreted the poem as being really about its own creation. Thus the very incoherence that either lends the poem a mysterious power or discredits the erring speaker becomes the inchoate energy, the fires and terrors, that the poem 'frames' into 'symmetry'. The divine blacksmith, with his furnace and hammer and anvil, is the poet, wrestling with recalcitrant images and his own fears and emerging not with answers but with a frame for the questions, which is enough for a successful poem. 'Frame' has a double meaning, both 'create' and 'limit': Blake had to control his energies as much as he stoked them. Some have added that, in defeating the questioner, the poem is announcing that it will defeat us, too, and the possible smile of the Tyger's creator – 'Did he smile his work to see?' – is a hint that the poem's creator is also smiling at the vain efforts of readers to grasp it. (Smiles are usually sinister in the *Songs*. Indeed some readers have seen, in certain copies, a smile on the drawn tiger.) It is a kind of nonsense poem, which toys with the conventions of meaning. If we think we have this tiger by the tail, we are bound to be mistaken, and in any case we had better let go and enjoy watching it romp. The very 'undecidability' of the text and design liberates us from being prisoners of any specific text, including the larger 'social texts' or ideologies of the real world.

As for the real world, some have argued that the Tyger represents the French Revolution, blazing into a particularly tigerish phase by 1793. Quite a few Britons, not all of them hostile to the Revolution as such, described it, or the mobs that kept pushing it to the political left, in tiger metaphors. On this reading, the poem's questioner becomes an appalled Englishman unable to fathom the depths of this social upheaval and unable to decide whether there could be any good in this manifest evil. Blake himself sometimes used similar imagery for revolutions, but it is one thing to see a tiger in the French Revolution and quite another to see the French Revolution in a tiger. There are tigers in the *Songs of Innocence,* after all, which could not allude to events in France, and it is hard to see how those events must alter our perceptions of a later member of the same species. It has yet to be shown that 'tiger' was used so frequently of the Revolution, and so infrequently of anything else, that a poem or picture of a tiger had to allude to it.

This sketch of recent readings of 'The Tyger' – and I am not going to offer a new one – may be discouraging, but at least it testifies to the continuing power of the poem. Something in it keeps attracting critics, with ever more powerful philosophical, linguistic or sociological theories, like moths to a flame. Some day we may find an adequate and convincing interpretation, but I rather doubt it; beyond a certain point the poem seems designed to resist interpretation. We may dispense, certainly, with any reading that smothers our initial impression of its incantatory power. But to grope like the Tyger's questioner for a comprehensive reading of the poem is a very good way into reading Blake as a whole. For there are many more tigers, blacksmiths and stars with spears, and there are many more situations or 'states' of perplexity that we are meant to pass through on our way to the vision of apocalypse at the end. We may regard this Tyger-induced bewilderment as one of the 'fallen' states, but we may also see it as itself apocalyptic, just one micro-second away from full revelation. To stand in awed bafflement before a terrible beast with yet more terrible implications may give that revelation the opening it needs into our imaginations. We are told in *The Four Zoas* that there was a time 'Where the lamb replies to the infant voice & the lion to the man of years / Giving them sweet instructions' ('Night the Sixth', page 71, lines 6–7). The Tyger says nothing to the questioner, but the poem, in provoking the questioner to such an insistent and vigorous imagining of the Tyger and its domain, not unlike the Zen master tormenting a novice into wisdom, rouses his faculties to act. When it sees he is ready, perhaps the Tyger will speak. Or perhaps it will not need to.

Before turning to 'London', we should note that some of the problems we have met in reading 'The Tyger' recur in other poems, such as 'The Sick Rose'. That poem, the briefest in *Experience,* is a gentler rendition of the situation in 'The Tyger', where a speaker encounters evil in nature and feels at a loss to explain it, and its very brevity generates endless irresolvable reverberations. We seem to be at dawn, after a stormy night, when the speaker discovers a cankered rose.

> O Rose thou art sick.
> The invisible worm,
> That flies in the night
> In the howling storm:
>
> Has found out thy bed
> Of crimson joy:
> And his dark secret love
> Does thy life destroy.

As an expression of shock and pity at the loss of an innocent and happy creature the poem is complete and satisfying enough. It has something of the simplicity of 'Spring' and 'Infant Joy' in *Innocence,* but simplicity surprised by death: *et in Arcadia ego.* The vivid image of the evil worm, 'invisible' because he does his work under cover of night and the noise of storms, like a thief or murderer, or indeed a rapist, dominates the mind of the speaker, who has now confronted the ravages of 'experience' in her garden. Unlike the speaker of 'The Tyger', she asks no questions about the purpose of the secret violence, and perhaps we should ask nothing further of the poem.

But the poem is so brief, its imagery so suggestive, even archetypal, that it is difficult to let it go; it will not let go of us. If Blake seems to reinvent the Christian pastoral world image by image in *Songs of Innocence,* here he has reimagined the Fall, when a serpent entered the Garden to seduce Eve, and death entered the world. He is almost restating Adam's speech when he learns what happened to Eve:

> How art thou lost, how on a sudden lost,
> Defac't, deflow'r'd, and now to Death devote?

> (*Paradise Lost,* Book IX, lines 900–901)

We no sooner think of Eve, however, when we wonder if the Rose herself is in any way at fault. Some critics have been hard on her and have compared her to the repressed old maids with sick, erotic day-dreams we find elsewhere in *Experience.* Some completely exonerate the worm, which is only a natural creature behaving quite naturally, or perhaps a phallic symbol responding healthily to the enticements of crimson joy. How did he come by his love, if she did not know him? Why did they not make love openly in the sunshine? Prompted by such thoughts (and seduced by Freud), such critics mine the poem with ironies. Much of this suspicion strikes me as blaming the victim, and with more than a touch of male supremacism, but it is hard to draw a line, in so resonant a poem, between what is really in the poem and what is not. No reading of the poem, at least, no matter how far it wanders among suggestions and suspicions, should abandon the initial impression of a beautiful flower, once filled with joy, blighted by a violent and surreptitious worm, just as no reading of 'The Tyger', no matter how many questions it throws back at the speaker, should lose the first experience of awe and fear before the Tyger itself.

'London'

If 'The Tyger' circles around a single sublime image with unanswered questions, 'London' steadily builds up increasingly comprehensive answers to its initial problem of why every face shows marks of weakness and woe. With its 'midnight streets', it is true, London is a forest of the night in which one may well wander, lost, but unlike the speaker of 'The Tyger' the city wanderer arrives somewhere by the end: at a vision that traces unhappy people to the institutions that oppress them and links all of them to 'mind-forg'd manacles'. George Orwell wrote in an essay: 'there is more understanding of the nature of capitalist society in a poem like "I wander through each charter'd street" than in three-quarters of Socialist literature'. This is a poem whose difficulties are due to compression rather than to radical uncertainty or ambiguity. If it is read carefully, it offers wider and deeper understanding with each stanza.

> I wander thro' each charter'd street,
> Near where the charter'd Thames does flow.
> And mark in every face I meet
> Marks of weakness, marks of woe.

It is possible to read the poem as a record of the speaker's growth of insight as he notices more symptoms and divines ever more comprehensive causes. Or we could read it as a kind of syllabus for us, arranged so as to conduct us most efficiently to the level of enlightenment achieved by the speaker. We follow him, in either case, from visible marks in faces, expressive of an unspecified weakness or woe, through auditory symptoms of mental chains, through sounds and their effects on the institutions that provoked them, and, finally, to a complex 'how' – how several victims are implicated in each other's destruction through several institutions. He does not proceed as a naïve empiricist might, noting sensory phenomena and sorting them into categories, for these are social facts, and he is not altogether a stranger to this society. He begins by stating a social fact fundamental to all the relationships he will describe: the streets and the Thames are chartered. An early draft of the poem in Blake's notebook has 'dirty street' and 'dirty Thames', but by changing the adjective to 'charter'd' Blake not only makes a more profound social claim (though dirt is a social fact too) but also intervenes in a debate over the meaning of charters that was reaching a peak in 1792, the year he most likely wrote the poem. For conservatives like Edmund Burke, charters are the sources of English rights and liberties; for radical reformers like Thomas Paine, charters are the 'musty records and moldy parchments' by which the dead inhibit the living. A charter may grant liberties to certain people, but at the same time it denies them to others. 'It is a perversion of terms,' Paine wrote in Part II of *The Rights of Man*, 'to say, that a charter gives rights. It operates by a contrary effect, that of taking rights away.'

Blake is certainly siding with Paine in this debate, but he also seems to signal the commercial sense of 'chartered' as 'leased' or 'hired'. Whole streets and the Thames itself are lined with commercial establishments – shops, wharves and warehouses – and the people are marked like branded slaves by the mercantile system that owns them. The marks are what Paine called the 'badges of ancient oppression'. When we look ahead to the victims named in the poem – chimney sweeper, soldier, harlot and wife – we see how 'charter'd' has prepared us to understand what they suffer in common. They are sold into slavery as chimney sweepers by their fathers, drafted into the army or navy for a few shillings, hired for a few hours as a harlot, or bought and sold on the London marriage market.

By repeating the word 'every' so insistently in the next stanza the speaker drives home the fact of misery's total permeation of society.

> In every cry of every Man,
> In every Infants cry of fear,
> In every voice: in every ban,
> The mind-forg'd manacles I hear[.]

There seems no escape; the manacles are in every mind. Some readers have taken another step and included the speaker in this universal disaster. How could his own mind be exempt? He admits to wandering and may therefore be lost, and his large claims may be just as much gropings in the dark as are the questions in 'The Tyger'. To push the poem any distance down this path, however, is to muffle or disperse what was manifest to Orwell, that it really does contain tremendous truths about modern society. Indeed part of the bleak power of the poem depends precisely on the speaker's solitariness: he alone sees things clearly. To take the poem's vision as itself a mark of mental weakness may seem to make things even bleaker, and therefore truer, but it also lands us in something like the Cretan paradox discussed earlier, for if the speaker has got things wrong, then perhaps not every mind is manacled after all – and then why should his be? We may believe that Blake ought to have been more self-conscious and ironic about his visionary powers (he in fact often despaired of them), but that belief gives us no right to assume that Blake undermines those powers when he displays them.

Blake's first notion of these famous manacles was anything but universal. In his notebook he wrote, 'The german forged links I hear' (Penguin edition, page 143), probably alluding to the German who sat on the English throne, George III, Elector of Hanover. Paine, in an updating of the 'Norman Yoke' idea, which held that William the Conqueror suppressed traditional English liberties, traced many of England's current ills to 'the coming of the Hanoverians'. In 1792 the radical London Corresponding Society, among whose large membership Blake doubtless had acquaintances, sent an address to the French National Assembly warning of German tyranny: 'Let German Despots act as they please, we shall rejoice at their fall; ... the King of Great Britain will do well to remember that this country is not Hanover.' In replacing 'german' with 'mind', Blake may have taken a more cautious course, but he also embraced a more difficult truth, for the evils of London are not political in a narrow sense but social, woven into the lives of all Londoners. If it were a matter of throwing off a foreign occupation, a brief uprising might be all that is necessary. We might even summon help from another foreigner, as we did in 1688, and as some radicals hoped we might do after 1793. But, as the women's movement has been asking in recent years, how do we fight an enemy who has outposts in our minds?

The first step, obviously, is to try to free our own minds and see things as they really are. The second, no less obviously, is to bring what we see home to other minds in vivid language and image. Hence

> How the Chimney-sweepers cry.
> Every blackning Church appalls,
> And the hapless Soldiers sigh,
> Runs in blood down Palace walls[.]

This language has a biblical ring and the images are apocalyptic. Like the parallel versets in Hebrew poetry, the two couplets present comparable young victims emitting sounds that leave their 'mark' on the comparable establishments that afflict them. The syntax of the first couplet seems to slip and slide under the burden of Blake's dense meanings, as we wonder what is appalling what and what is blackening what. 'Blackning' might be intransitive, telling us that churches grow black, literally and figuratively, in the London air. Taken transitively, its object must be the chimney sweeper, whose task it sometimes is, of course, to remove the black from the churches' own chimneys. By sanctioning the practice of sending little boys up chimneys the Church has not only failed in its duty to protect God's children but has blackened their minds with mysterious justifications of things as they are, making up a heaven of their misery. And the blackened little boys that emerge from the chimneys become the sacrificial victims under the dismal shade of mystery.

As I stated earlier, 'appalls' as an active verb had connotations lost in the more frequent modern use in the passive voice. 'I am appalled' usually means 'I am shocked and indignant', but the churches are hardly indignant here (assuming that 'Every ... Church' is the object of the verb, and not the subject, which is possible but forced). To appall, as I have said, literally means to make pale or strike with pallor, to frighten so that the blood drains from the face. I think we are to imagine each church turning pale with guilt at the cry of the sweeper – 'weep, weep' – while turning black with sin at having blessed his 'duty'. In a less complex but equally intense parallel image, the palace turns red at the death-sigh of a soldier, no doubt conscripted while still a youth to fight in America or in India or – soon – in France, against other youths with whom he has no personal quarrel. The blood flowing from his wounds turns into a kind of handwriting on the palace walls, a sign of the sin committed by the man of blood inside.

The notebook drafts indicate that Blake had first planned to end his poem with the third stanza, but, having wandered for another night, perhaps, through the woeful sounds of London, he returned to the poem to write an even more comprehensive epitome of what he heard.

> But most thro' midnight streets I hear
> How the youthful Harlots curse
> Blasts the new-born Infants tear
> And blights with plagues the Marriage hearse[.]

As the 'curse' is another in the series of cries, we might expect another couplet describing how this sound affects the structure that evokes it, and that, in part, is what we find. As the cry appalls each church, and the sigh bloodies the palace, so the curse blights the institution of marriage, which Blake brilliantly embodies in a 'hearse' that would seem to carry the newly-weds to their death. Marriage is itself the business of both Church and State, and it is a business in the commercial sense as well. So is harlotry, of course, and indeed it was one of the chief occupations for London women in the 1790s. 'What is a Wife & what is a Harlot?' Blake later asks, 'are they Two and not One? can they Exist Separate?' (*Jerusalem*, plate 57, lines 8 and 9). His answer is no: they are alike in being exploited commercially for the purposes of men, and they are opposite sides of the same coin. You cannot have virtuous and virginal brides ready to assume the roles expected of them in Hanoverian England – where marriages are arranged and passionless, and divorce nearly impossible – without also having a large society of whores to provide a sexual outlet.

It is not only the institution of marriage that is blighted, however, for this triplet also tells, in the bleakest line of the poem, how the harlot's curse 'Blasts the new-born Infants tear'. What does this mean? The

49

blast could be the breath escaping the harlot when she curses the 'Marriage hearse'. We might imagine her screaming, 'A plague on you!' as a wedding party drives past, and blowing away the frightened tears from the cheeks of the baby she holds in her arms. Or, since she does not want the baby, she might be cursing it for its cry of woe. But 'blast' as verb or noun also connotes disease or blight; since biblical times diseases were thought to be borne on the wind. Some critics have questioned this interpretation, but it seems inescapable that the lines also imply venereal disease. It was known in Blake's day that a form of gonorrhoea could infect babies at birth and cause blindness within weeks. An early manuscript fragment contains a line that reads like a comment on this passage: 'swift as the Nightly Blast that Blights the Infant Bud' (E 448); the same imagery, we saw, is found in 'The Sick Rose'. So the harlot's midnight business curses her baby, and not only hers but her client's bride's baby as well, for she transmits her plagues to all her customers and their families. The image of the infant blighted in its birth is echoed in the poem's final phrase, in which a wedding carriage is transformed into a funeral hearse.

There is a great deal more that could be said about this wonderful and terrifying poem, but we shall leave it here. The best place to read it is in the pavement on the south side of the Thames a little north of Westminster Bridge – the 'Silver Jubilee Walkway' – where you can look across at the Houses of Parliament and the Ministry of Defence buildings between stanzas. Blake would have been impressed by the wisdom of the Greater London Council in having it chiselled into the pavement 'that all may read'; he would have smiled to see that after two more centuries London had finally planted the seeds of its own redemption.

Are there signs of hope or redemption in the poem itself? Some readers have found a kind of bracing clarity in being made to face the interlocked horrors of the city in such unrelieved bleakness, as if we have reached what Blake later called the 'Limit of Opakeness' and the 'Limit of Contraction' and can only rise and expand from here. But that is not much of a consolation. Some readers have found in the design for the poem a hint or two that renovation is possible. For in each of the two scenes depicted there is a little boy, usually dressed in green, and in one of them at least he is offering the kind of aid or comfort nowhere suggested in the text. At the top a boy leads an old man on crutches, perhaps blind, towards a doorway; the boy looks up at the old man and at a light shining upon them from above. In the lower scene the same boy or a similar one warms his hands at an enormous smoky fire. We may imagine little tales to account for these pictures, as we imagine stories of harlots and babies to account for the final stanza. The man and boy, or boys, may all be victims marked by weakness and woe, but there is also something of the warmth and solace of the chimney sweeper of *Innocence* and his little friend Tom Dacre. The upper scene brings to mind the line from Isaiah 11:6, 'and a little child shall lead them', which foretells the coming of the Redeemer. So I like to imagine Blake drafting a fifth stanza, such as

> Through these wintry streets and wild
> Through this Babylon, through this Tyre
> Clad in green a little child
> Leads an old man to his fire.

A stanza which he wisely left out, though a little of its spirit appears in the design. The New Jerusalem always hovers over the fallen city.

3. The Book of Thel

For what is your life? It is even a vapour, that appeareth for a little time, and then vanisheth away.

> (James 4:14)

In Selfhood we are nothing: but fade away in mornings breath.

> (Blake, *Jerusalem*, plate 40, line 13)

Tend the flock of God that is your charge, not by constraint but willingly ... And when the chief Shepherd is manifested you will obtain the unfading crown of glory.

> (I Peter 5:2–4)

Thel is the youngest daughter of 'Mne Seraphim', but she is also the youngest of a larger sisterhood that includes Lyca, Ona and the 'maiden Queen' of *Songs of Experience* and Oothoon of *Visions of the Daughters of Albion*. Blake seems to have found their common situation deeply interesting, both for what it can be made to show about different states of mind and for what it can be made to convey as a vehicle for wider allegorical meanings. Lyca surmounts her parents' fears and enters a realm of sleep or the imagination where beasts of prey gambol about her and lick her and take her naked to their cave; her parents follow her 'vision' and learn to fear no more. Ona's limbs shake with terror at the end, when she confronts her frightened father, but she has at least learned to forget her fear long enough to delight naked with the bright youth. Oothoon, as we shall see, starts her life trembling and woeful, but soon rises up boldly and flies to her lover. Thel also begins trembling and woeful, but her first venture outside the vales of Har so frightens her that she flees back to their protection. We envisage her at the end as having come to the same state as the 'maiden Queen' (Thel is also called a maiden and a queen) who resists the angel of the title and hides from him her heart's delight: she will become a bitter old maid with grey hairs on her head. The story of Thel is sufficiently complex, however, that many of its readers have felt unable to condemn its heroine for her final retreat.

Blake engraved '1789' on the title-page of *The Book of Thel*, the same date he gave to *Songs of Innocence*, and it is clear that the vales of

Har are indeed a world of innocence, at least as the 'Lilly', 'Cloud' and 'Clod of Clay' see them. The place outside the vales, the 'land unknown' where Thel finds 'her own grave plot' (plate 6, lines 2 and 9) certainly resembles the world of experience, and in fact the manner of engraving in both text and design suggests we should date plate 6 or section IV two years later (along with the mysterious 'Motto'), when Blake was working on *Songs of Experience*. It may be that when Blake completed the first five plates or first three sections, he had not decided Thel's fate. As she has not yet responded to the invitation of 'matron Clay' to enter her house, Blake might have had her decline to do so as she has declined the less explicit invitations of the Lilly and Cloud. He might on the other hand have sent Thel forth, encouraged by the Clod of Clay's counsel to 'fear nothing', and let her find miseries as well as the strength to overcome them. Instead he did give her the courage to enter in and wander about, but it fails her when she hears the voice from her grave. He thereby created a more satisfying climax than the first option, and added interest by making her virgin fears more explicit. The outcome of the second option he reserves for his much braver heroine Oothoon.

Blake's Mythology

Before following Thel more closely through her education in the vales of Har (and outside them), we shall stop to face what many readers find the most intimidating and exasperating feature of Blake's longer poems on first reading them: the strange names of people and places. In *The Book of Thel* we have not only the heroine's name but Mne Seraphim (in the first line), Adona, Har, Luvah and 'the northern bar'. Many editions of Blake, or commentaries on Blake, confidently identify the names, either by providing an etymology or by invoking the late epic prophecies, where Luvah, for instance, who is merely mentioned in *Thel*, has a major part. Newcomers to Blake's work are no doubt grateful for such help, which at least gets them past the names and on to the events and situations, themselves often difficult enough to understand. But such help may do as much harm as good, as most identifications rest on debatable assumptions, and they breed a misleading comfort through an easy familiarity. Since *Thel* is a separate work, published separately, we have no warrant for assuming that a name such as Luvah must 'mean' what the same name means in another work (written ten or more years later, moreover); once you start wheeling in Blake's later epic machinery, you may crush what is unique in *Thel*. It is also very questionable whether a consciously invented name can be said to have

53

an etymology in the way a natural language has. In coining new ones, Blake may have been alluding to traditional myths, but he may have also been trying to free himself, and us, from all traditional associations and make a fresh beginning. The very strangeness of the names may be part of their 'meaning'.

We meet a strange, though partly familiar, name in the opening line: 'The daughters of Mne Seraphim led round their sunny flocks'. Now Blake was an admirer of the poems of 'Ossian', the ancient Gaelic bard whose songs James Macpherson had recently claimed to have recovered and translated from Highland singers who knew them. None of the songs contains a rounded story like those of Homer, to whom Ossian was regularly compared, and some of them seem mere fragments of an epic cycle. They usually begin in the midst of things and presume their hearer knows who the characters are. For example, a poem entitled *Fingal* begins, 'Cuchullin sat by Tura's wall', and the next two pages give a dozen more proper names. I think Macpherson may provide Blake's precedent for this effect. Like many readers, Blake enjoyed the very strangeness of the Ossianic names and, unlike Macpherson, he does not help to dispel the effect with explanatory footnotes. He wants us to feel that we are entering a new world, or perhaps a primal world older than Ossian, Homer and even the Bible, where there are few familiar landmarks.

Once we take in the little shiver of exotic or cosmic depths the names induce and prepare ourselves for something unprecedented, what are we to make of the names themselves? Perhaps nothing at all. 'Thel' seems almost a blank to be filled in after we see her in action, an algebraic *x* whose value we derive from the formulae in which it appears. 'Har' seems similarly minimal and free of associations. Of course there has been no end of scholarly guessing. 'Har' turns out to be Hebrew for 'mountain' and the name of a wise king in the Icelandic Edda. Nearly every commentary claims that 'Thel' derives from the Greek *thelos* – 'will' or 'wish' – because an influential Blake scholar said so once and no one has a convincing alternative. It can seem apt enough for the wistful Thel once one has thought of it, but it is less apt than another Greek word, *thelus*, which means 'female', as well as 'fresh' and 'gentle'. Yet Blake does not seem to have known Greek in 1789, and neither source is likely to have been triggered in the minds of his readers even if they knew Greek (though an odd coinage, *thely-phthora,* meaning 'destruction of females', was circulating in the titles of poems by Martin Madan and William Cowper).

A little more likely as a recognizable allusion would be Thalia, the

Muse who (sometimes) represents the pastoral. Thel is a shepherdess, as we see in the title-page illustration, and her poem is a kind of pastoral elegy. The pastoral elegy was originally a lament for the dying Adonis, here made feminine as Adona, the river beside which Thel laments her own dying. Whatever else 'Mne Seraphim' may mean, the 'Mne' suggests 'Mnemosyne', mother of the Muses. These associations carry us somewhat farther than the other Greek 'etymologies', but they do not bring much to the poem we could not infer without them.

If we turn the idea of etymology around, however, we may find a fruitful way to approach Blake's strange new names. They are not to be derived from Greek or Hebrew or Scots Gaelic, but the reverse: they themselves are the original words from which the Greek, Hebrew and Scots Gaelic words are derived. Their echo of familiar words, their air of 'etymologicity', comes from an assertion of priority, as if they belonged to the first language on earth. Blake seems to have accepted the widely held view, not yet displaced by the new science of historical linguistics, that Hebrew was the original language, though sometimes he suggests that Hebrew was the earliest derivative of a language that was earlier still. By this theory, 'Thel' would be the pre-Hebrew root of, say, Thalia, *thelos, thelus, tellus* (Latin for 'earth'), *thal* (Hebrew for 'dew') and everything else Blake scholars may come up with. We are invited to view the world of *Thel*, then, almost as Thel herself does, as a pristine place where the psychological and mythical action is fundamental to human life. To maintain this view, we should not let all the possible meanings and sources of the names erase their initial strangeness.

Thel's Retreat

Thel is a shepherdess who has abandoned her part in her sisterhood's duty in order to lament the transience of her life. Just why she leaves the sunny flocks, just why this grief comes over her, we are never told, but there is more than a hint that her departure from the sunny realm brings about the very mortality she laments. In spatial terms her path is certainly a descent or fall through the four elements, from the empyrean realm of divine light and fire, which in her 'paleness' she seems unable to bear, through the 'secret' (unlit) air, 'down' to a shady river valley, and eventually to earth – the 'Clod of Clay'. When she hears her own voice at the end speak of a 'youthful burning boy' (plate 6, line 19) she has come full circle, but she flees this fiery encounter as she fled the sun at the outset. As we circle back ourselves, we can see that she has been avoiding something sexual all along. Though it is not even implicit in the beginning, we can see that she has divorced herself from a kind of marriage to the sun, whom we might tentatively call Luvah.

Thel weeps over her mortality, her transience, the senselessness of being 'born to smile & fall' (plate 1, line 7). After talking with the Cloud, she adds a second complaint, that she is 'without a use' (plate 3, line 22), which at first seems distinct from the question of mortality. The chief moral of the poem, however, is that these two problems are really one. The creatures Thel questions all preach the unity of life, the integration of each creature's 'use' into a circle. They give lessons in ecology. The cycle of vegetation, of water, even the digestive cycle are fully represented. Each thing dies only to be 'used' by another thing, which in turn gives itself up to a third. The first thing comes back in its season, yet, even when consumed by another, each creature undergoes not death but transfiguration.

Thel sees that the Lilly gives away her 'breath' to those who lack it, 'those that cannot crave [ask or beg], the voiceless, the o'ertired' (plate 2, line 4). Her perfume transforms the grass on which she scatters it into nourishment for the milked cow, who has given away her own substance to a calf or child. The lamb even 'crops' the Lilly while she cheerfully serves herself up as both food and napkin (plate 2, lines 6–7). The Cloud, who presents himself next, is not explicitly consumed, but he is just as generous, scattering his bright beauty and 'bearing food to all our tender flowers'. He is even more ephemeral than the Lilly, and indeed is almost identical to the perfume she disperses. The Clod of Clay then appears, and, bending over a weeping worm, 'her life exhai'd / In milky fondness' (plate 4, lines 8–9). Because she gives her own breath away as the Lilly does, her suckling of the worm, if that is what 'milky' implies, is just as self-sacrificing. The Clod, of course, is the end of the life cycle, 'the food of worms' (plate 3, line 23), to which we come at death, as Thel has unhappily observed. Lilies and grass will pass through cows, cows themselves will pass into dust and dung. 'Imperious Caesar, dead and turn'd to clay,' Hamlet says, 'Might stop a hole to keep the wind away,' but what Hamlet terms the 'base uses' to which we are put when reduced to clay are celebrated as 'great' by the Cloud. His speech to Thel is like Gabriel's Annunciation to Mary:

> Then if thou art the food of worms, O virgin of the skies,
> How great thy use, how great thy blessing; every thing that lives,
> Lives not alone, nor for itself: fear not . . .

> (plate 3, lines 25–7)

The Clod of Clay, as death and the source of life, as end and beginning, epitomizes the life cycle or 'use' cycle that Thel has been studying. The Clod is the pivot, which is why she contains the 'eternal gates' (plate 6, line 1). One can enter and return, as she says, yet one returns, it seems, not by turning back, as Thel does, but by going steadily forward, 'fearing not'. The cycle will bring one back round again through a rebirth only if one undergoes the seeming death of giving everything away to others.

Some readers have argued that Thel is perfectly justified in resisting the lesson that the creatures teach, for she is not a natural object like a lily or a cloud but a human being, or at least a human consciousness, and perhaps an angel. Nor does she have a 'use' in the way a thing does: in Kant's terms, she is an end, not a means. It is all very well for Blake, or Thel herself, to endow nature with human forms and speech, but in 'real' nature lilies and clouds are not conscious of their life or their death and cannot be said to be generous or self-sacrificing or full of love. The 'eternal vales' that the creatures faithfully expect to enjoy after they melt or evaporate are not the eternity we see in nature. When a flower dies, a new one springs up, and to us they are the same flower; that is one sort of eternity. Another sort is a flower's participation in the eternal totality of nature: Blake's 'Lilly' survives, though entirely transformed, in the body of the lamb, and then again as the lamb becomes clay, and as the clay becomes milk for worms, and so on. Neither of these notions of eternity can accommodate consciousness, however, or individuality as we usually conceive of it. What is uniquely human, or angelic, will be irremediably lost, and the poem really is a kind of elegy, if not tragedy.

I think, however, that not only the three creatures but the poem itself speaks eloquently against Thel's viewpoint, and only a perversely suspicious reading, or one that confuses real girls with girls in poems, could so discredit the consensus of the creatures as to justify Thel's shrieking flight back to the vales of Har. To argue the irrelevance of a lesson based on flowers and clouds, first of all, is to argue the irrelevance of the Sermon on the Mount. Jesus tells us there to 'consider the lilies': though they live brief lives, God arrays them more gloriously than Solomon, so we, like them, should take no thought for the morrow. The Lilly in *Thel,* in fact, is one of the same lilies, and her sermon is a little Sermon on the Mount. Nor does Jesus shrink from using natural imagery elsewhere – not only in his parables, which are similes, but at the Last Supper, where he is more profoundly metaphorical. We are to eat and drink the body and blood of Christ, and in his death we live.

57

We are free to reject this command, of course, as we are free to say that real human beings are fundamentally unlike flowers or lambs, but we are not free to say Jesus did not mean what he said or that Blake's mode of teaching implicitly exempts human beings.

It is not obvious, either, that Thel is so different from the creatures she questions. As an experiment in reading the poem it would be worth trying out the idea that Thel is a dewdrop or cloud of dew, no different from the 'fair eyed dew' whom the Cloud courts on 'balmy flowers' (plate 3, lines 12 and 13). Many of her movements can be 'naturalized' in this way. More to the point, however, is the definition of consciousness or individuality that Thel's defenders implicitly adopt. Thel's brand of individuality seems to resemble what Blake terms 'Selfhood' and which he constantly urges us to discard. Thel is very self-regarding, as one of her first similes for herself, 'reflection in a glass' (plate 1, line 9) should alert us. She is also self-objectifying, exemplified by her habit of calling herself 'Thel' and of seeing herself as she imagines (wrongly) others will see her: 'who shall find my place' (plate 2, line 12); 'no one hears my voice'; 'And all shall say, without a use this shining woman liv'd' (plate 3, lines 4 and 22). To see ourselves as others see us may seem to be at one remove from our Selfhoods, but it is not an entry into the circle of altruism; it is a short circuit through abstract others back to ourselves. Thel has little interest in the interior life of those others, so the self she projects back on to herself via their perceptions is mostly exterior, a matter of 'place' or 'voice'. It is like looking into a mirror, where the 'I' that looks in is not given a greeting of the spirit but is confronted by the face of an 'other' that both sees and is the outside of the 'I'. What a mirror gives us, what the opinion of others gives us, is not permanence and solidity which are impossible, but that defensive illusion of permanence and solidity which is precisely what Blake means by Selfhood. Thel wants to become the Pebble, who seemed to have the last word against the Clod of Clay in *Experience,* but what she ought to become is the Clod of Clay, whose consciousness embraces so wide a world, and whose individuality is composed of so many others, that when she is trampled by a cow she is happy for the cow and genuinely forgetful of her 'self'. Or if Thel could acquire that ready sense of identification with other creatures that the speaker of 'The Fly' shows (also in *Experience*) – 'Am not I / A fly like thee? / Or art thou not / A man like me?' – she would find, as he does, that death holds no terrors.

There is another theme, however, that may make all this more intelligible and will in any case bring us back to the burning boy, the turning point in Thel's career and the crucial point in the case for or against her retreat. The Lilly speaks of her morning visitor in terms metaphorical for the sun as well as traditional for God.

> I am visited from heaven. and he that smiles on all.
> Walks in the valley. and each morn over me he spreads his hand.

(plate 1, lines 19–20)

He promises her a kind of exaltation in this life – 'thou shalt be clothed in light, and fed with morning manna' – and another exaltation or eternal flowering in the next one, after she is melted by the 'summers heat'. That heat can only be his own, and she looks forward to it. Manna was traditionally taken to be a kind of dew; this dew is warm with God's love, resembling what Shelley in the poem 'Epipsychidion' called the 'fiery dews that melt / Into the bosom of a frozen bud'. The erotic dimension of the Lilly's relationship to the sun is seconded by allusions to the Book of Revelation, where the faithful few who walk with Christ are 'clothed in white' and receive 'the hidden manna' (3:4–5, 2:17). Those so clothed and fed comprise the new Church that will be invited to the wedding supper of the Lamb: 'For the marriage of the Lamb is come, and his wife hath made herself ready' (19:7). When we come to Blake's 'innocent lamb' and his cropping of the smiling Lilly (plate 2, lines 5–6), it is hard, with Revelation in mind, not to think of the Lamb's wedding supper; the lines are certainly erotic.

The imagery surrounding the Cloud is much more explicitly marital, though it seems that the Cloud, not God, is the groom. The Cloud who descends at Thel's complaint is filled with sunlight: he is bright and glittering and golden-headed. His steeds drink of the same golden springs as Luvah's horses – that is, the dew as it arises from flowers and grass. So in some sense the Cloud is an ambassador of the sun, or his immanent presence, perhaps, like the gilded butterfly that perches on the Lilly. The Cloud tells how he descends to the flowers and courts the dew so that she will take him into her shining tent, though not before they are properly married – 'never [to] part' (plate 3, line 15) – with the morning sun officiating. If the Cloud is a surrogate for the sun, the 'fair eyed' but 'weeping virgin' dew is a stand-in for Thel. Thel seems not to have . noticed his oblique proposal, however, and contrasts herself with him on the grounds of her uselessness. She cannot see, or cannot admit, that the 'use' to which she is being called is not limited to the cycle of vegetation but includes a transfiguring marriage to God.

What is only suggested in the Lilly's speech, and somewhat displaced if more explicit in the Cloud's, emerges with full clarity in the Clod of Clay's. The Clod tells Thel: 'he that loves the lowly. pours his oil upon my head. / And kisses me, and binds his nuptial bands around my breast' (plate 5, lines 1–2). These lines still refer metaphorically to the sun and its beams of light, yet they apply much more overtly to the divine marriage of God with the earth, the land of Israel (as described in Isaiah or Hosea), or of Christ with the Church of the faithful, with the individual Christian soul, or with the Virgin Mother. He calls the Clod the 'mother of my children' and tells her he has given her 'a crown that none can take away' (plate 5, lines 3 and 4), which is the crown that Christ tells the faithful to hold fast to (Revelation 3:11) and the crown that Peter mentions in language (quoted at the beginning of this chapter) that almost summarizes the situation of Thel herself. By the second line of the poem, Thel has left her sunny flocks and her own glory is fading. The three creatures with whom she talks all tell the same tale – by precept and example, and with increasing explicitness – that by selfless love one will attain an intimate union, a marriage, with the sunlike Christ.

The final plate of *Thel* begins with the 'eternal gates terrific porter' and the 'northern bar'. We cannot rely on Blake's punctuation to tell us whether there is more than one eternal gate, but it is natural to imagine that the vales of Har have at least two, one at the north and one at the south. Various esoteric sources have been offered for such gates, but within the poem itself we need only ask what would have happened had she gone out of the southern gate. There she would have met the sun, and perhaps returned to the mountain top and to her flocks. By going north she simply continues her flight from the sun into cooler and darker spaces. Hades is traditionally set in the north or north-west (where the sun sets); indeed in the *Odyssey* it is situated in a land of clouds where the sun never shines.

Here Thel hears the 'voice of sorrow' from her own 'grave plot':

> Why cannot the Ear be closed to its own destruction?
> Or the glistening Eye to the poison of a smile!

And so it continues until it reaches the 'burning boy' and the 'little curtain of flesh on the bed of our desire' (plate 6, lines 11–20). These lines differ sharply in content and tone from the rest of the poem, but I think they are none the less dramatically and logically fitting. If we note that the lesson about 'use' and its recompense which the creatures preach is always expressed in sexual and marital terms, then we may recognize the initially rather mysterious final speech as a culmination and revelation of what Thel has been shrinking from all along. It may also seem to be a narrowing of the theme, since the sexual dimension of the creatures' activity does not absorb or cancel the themes of feeding and nursing, scattering and evaporating, cherishing and wiping away taints. If it is a narrowing, it is a reflection of Thel's restricted notion of what sexuality is. If the Lilly, who is clothed and melted, cropped and scattered, is 'polymorphously perverse', in psychoanalytic terms, then Thel has made a fetish of genital sex. Ideal or unfallen sexuality may be something like what Milton's angels enjoy: they 'obstacle find none / Of membrane, joint, or limb, exclusive bars' (*Paradise Lost*, Book VIII, lines 624–5). For them there is no curb or curtain of flesh, the penetration of which so frightens Thel. 'Embraces are Cominglings,' Blake adds, 'from the Head even to the Feet' (*Jerusalem*, plate 69, line 43). The way to achieve such an ideal is by going through the strait gate of sexual desire that our fallen condition permits, not by avoiding any contact whatsoever.

The anguished questions of the voice of sorrow, which we may interpret as Thel's own projected voice, dwell on the five senses and the experiences that threaten them. These are the five windows that light the fallen 'caverned' man, as Blake put it later, whereas once upon a time man possessed enlarged and numerous senses (*Europe*, plate iii, line 1; *The Marriage of Heaven and Hell*, plate 11). Thel in her retreat from the sun-filled realm of the Seraphim, we may imagine, has sealed off her numerous senses one by one until only five remain, and reduced her 'polymorphous' sexuality to a secret place behind a curtain. She has looked askance and asquint at the lessons of the creatures, as if between 'Eyelids stord with arrows ready drawn', in the words of her grave-plot voice. As such a defensive sceptic, she will never find the faith of the creatures, which is 'the evidence of things not seen' (Hebrews 11:1), and she will see the youthful burning boy as merely a bringer of her pain and destroyer of her virginity, rather than the fulfilment of her proper 'use' and the incarnate form of the divine sun of her state of innocence.

The Designs

Most of the designs do not call up ideas that we cannot derive from the text alone, but the first and the last go beyond the text and are richly suggestive. On the title-page, Thel's posture, which is not only upright and aloof but even averted from the amorous flowers so that she must look askance or even backwards to watch them, nicely catches her stance or standpoint throughout the poem as that of the wallflower at the dance of nature. The red flowers, perhaps anemones or Adonis flowers, are the site of the Cloud's forthright courtship of the dew. In size and attitude, both physical and mental, these lovers contrast with Thel in just the same way as the tiny figures above them contrast with the chaste and upright characters of Thel's name, which they are climbing and playing on as if it were a jungle gym. Thel must feel put upon. But these severe Roman letters seem to be chiselled on to the marble face of a tombstone outlined by the arching willow. The willow is a traditional graveside tree, because it seems to weep, as Thel does, and it has long been an emblem for chastity and in particular for virgins who have lost their lovers or who, like Thel, never find them. According to Spenser in the *Faerie Queene,* the willow is 'worne of forlorne Paramours'. It grows beside rivers, like the river of Adona in the poem, an association that calls to mind the rivers of Babylon by which the daughters of Zion wept, having hung their harps upon the willows (Psalm 137). It is in a 'weeping brook' with a willow over it that the chaste Ophelia, who lost her lover, let herself drown. Thel, passively suicidal like Ophelia, watches a young couple enact what she has renounced, in front of a tombstone with her name on it. The gist of the action and the moral of the story are contained in this one design.

The design on the final plate, a great sinuous serpent tamely allowing a girl to rein and ride it with her two little brothers, a scene not illustrating any passage in the poem, solicits an act of imaginative interpretation on our part. Is this another little group in the vales of Har who would have preached the same lesson had Thel encountered them? Is this the infant worm, cherished by the Clod of Clay, now grown to maturity and taking, say, a new and more trusting Thel for a ride? Other possibilities suggest themselves, but they all point to a realm of innocence where lions lie down with lambs. In fact the chapter of Isaiah that describes this realm, which I cited as a possible presence in the design of 'London', also contains three children who rather neatly correspond to the three children here: the 'little child' who leads the lion, wolf and leopard with their former prey, the lamb, kid and calf; the 'sucking child' who plays harmlessly over the hole of the asp; and the 'weaned child' who put his hand without hurt on the den of the cockatrice, a serpent (Isaiah 11:6–8). Blake alludes to this passage in his early play *King Edward the Third,* where the Prince likens his reck-lessness to 'the innocent child' who, 'Unthinking, plays upon the viper's den' (scene [3], lines 241–2). If we are meant to think of this passage, and the allusion is hard to resist, then the design becomes a little revelation of the unfallen or restored realm, the 'married land' Thel could have belonged to. It is not very different from the land the creatures have always known, but now it embraces the natural predators who had never entered the vales of Har until, perhaps, Thel conjured them up out of her fears. The picture, then, occupies a kind of conditional space: if Thel had acknowledged the leopard and asp and cockatrice – animal forms of the human aggressors the voice relays to her by the grave plot – as harmful only to her defensive Selfhood, she would be living now in a larger and even more generous and loving world.

4. Towards Revolution

To see '1789' engraved on the title-pages of *Songs of Innocence* and *The Book of Thel* is to sense a more poignant fragility in the gentle, loving world of innocence than we might have felt if we were not aware of the thunder just outside the vales. That is not to say that the world before the French Revolution was in any sense innocent. On the contrary, Blake felt as millions of others did that something like a long-lost innocence might *return* to the public sphere through the Revolution and its hoped-for counterparts in England and elsewhere. The word 'revolution' had not yet lost its older sense of a restoration of an original liberty that had been usurped by a tyrant. Yet after 1789 Blake seldom sounded the notes we hear among the pipers and infants and lilies and clods, except as brief episodes within much larger stories filled with trumpets and drums, pleas and boasts, groans and lamentations. Perhaps we can attribute the desperate tone and harsh imagery in the voice from Thel's grave plot to Blake's new confrontation with social evils newly illuminated by revolutionary possibility. That is even more likely to be the case with the *Songs of Experience,* especially those poems that deal with the evils (such as black servitude and child labour) that the Revolution seemed ready to eradicate.

Blake took up the French Revolution as a subject with little delay. In 1791 the first of the seven proposed books of *The French Revolution: A Poem* was set up in type and at least one proof printed. It takes the story from the convening of the Estates General and the dismissal of Necker to the withdrawal of the royal army from Paris. Why it was never published we do not know, nor have the other six books ever turned up. 'A Song of Liberty', which concludes *The Marriage of Heaven and Hell* (begun in 1790, published in 1793), alludes to the destruction of the Bastille and ends with 'the son of fire' rising in the east and shouting 'Empire is no more'. After the withdrawal of *The French Revolution,* however, Blake seemed to stand back in order to take a wider and longer view. *Visions of the Daughters of Albion,* published in 1793, certainly registers a revolutionary mood, but the oppressed daughters of Albion look to America, not France, for liberation. Blake then turned to *America: A Prophecy* (also 1793) and finally returned to contemporary events with *Europe: A Prophecy* (1794); he linked these two by prefixing each with a 'Preludium', and then 'enclosed' them both in a wider, four-continent survey of events from the Fall of Adam to the general resurrection. 'Africa' and 'Asia' comprised parts one and four of his fourfold visionary history, though these two parts were then bound together in *The Song of Los* in 1795.

In this chapter we will look at *Visions of the Daughters of Albion* and *America: A Prophecy*. Before we do this, however, we might look again briefly at *Thel,* to see if that poem prepares us at all for the grand political and social themes of those that follow it. I think it does so in a number of ways. The basic situation or configuration presented in the poem – a young woman, her real or potential lover, the rising or setting of the sun, her relations with 'nature' or natural creatures – is one to which Blake returns again and again. As it expands in later poems to include vast historical events on several continents, Blake seems less to think *about* this situation than to think *through* it or *with* it. It becomes a visionary instrument.

Blake makes clear at the opening of *Visions of the Daughters of Albion* that its heroine, Oothoon, is a 'Contrary' of Thel in character. The creation of a contrary of Thel need not extend the poem's symbolic limits beyond those established in *Thel* – as Lyca does not in 'The Little Girl Lost' and 'The Little Girl Found' – but no sooner is the heroine of *Visions* introduced in a *Thel*-like setting than she is made to represent the soul of America, black slavery and the oppressed women of the world. Thel and Oothoon are recast again as the 'shadowy female' of both *America* and *Europe,* and indeed the Enitharmon of the latter work has a great deal of Thel in her. The 'youthful burning boy' of Thel's anticlimax reappears as Orc in *America* and *Europe,* after a detour into Oothoon's joint oppressors, Bromion and Theotormon. Orc is sunlike, rising at the dawn of revolution; Enitharmon is Thel-like and prefers night-time. Flowers speak to Oothoon as they do to Thel, but the 'shadowy female' is assimilated to nature itself and lapses into silence. These and many other transpositions are traceable through all of Blake's later works, and to follow them in sequence is one of the best ways to gain a purchase on their increasing complexities.

A more important service to a reader's preparation for them is *Thel*'s celebration of the heroic selflessness of the Lilly, Cloud and Clod of Clay. Perfect exemplars of fraternity and mutual aid, Blake presents them not only as an implied condemnation of the doctrine of possessive individualism, no longer shame-faced thanks to *laissez-faire* economic theory, but as a summons for us to emulate them in this life, indeed as a kind of prophecy of the social renovation Blake was to see in the French Revolution. To try to live like the self-sacrificing little creatures may seem preposterous even to social revolutionaries, but Blake invites us to do so in absolute earnest throughout his writings. His character Milton, for instance, comes to understand the difference between his own incomplete revolutionary role during the Commonwealth and the genuinely renovative acts that he is capable of. To Satan, who is part of himself, he says

> Thy purpose & the purpose of thy Priests & of thy Churches
> Is to impress on men the fear of death; to teach
> Trembling & fear, terror, constriction; abject selfishness
> Mine is to teach Men to despise death & to go on
> In fearless majesty annihilating Self . . .

> *(Milton,* plate 38, lines 37–41)

If we can see Milton here as a Lilly or Cloud aroused to prophetic indignation against an enemy, we can equally see the Lilly or Cloud as possessing a 'fearless majesty' that we might not have thought to look for. The difference between Milton and the Lilly comes of the fact that the serpent has not yet entered the garden of the creatures of Har and, in any case, would have no effect on them: the Lilly and her fellows are still innocent, but their very innocence is so manifestly perfect that no serpent would corrupt them. This is not the case with Thel, and indeed by retreating back into the vales of Har she will in a sense have brought the serpent with her, the serpent of the Selfhood she is so desperate to preserve. By then, however, she and the creatures will inhabit different spaces, they still in their garden of mutual delight, she in a desert no longer distinguishable from the dark 'land of sorrows'.

What Blake most admired in the Revolution, as did the great French historian Michelet after him, was the self-sacrifice and unification of the people, the acts that the creatures of *Thel* preach and practise. The creatures lack the motive of a common enemy, it is true, and its absence may be one reason why the poem seems so fragile, but Blake considers it no different from the more robust fraternity of the people in arms – who, after all, envisaged a day when all enemies would join in a universal confederation. Two terms in Milton's speech, 'abject' and 'majesty', have obvious social connotations. When His Majesty the King was eliminated from the French nation, abjectness was eliminated too, but majesty was transferred to the people. Abjectness, in its social as well as individual guise, is really selfishness, or fearful self-preservation. Majesty, as a king or God embodies it, is the projection of one's abject self on to a collective other, but as an attribute of the people it is the willing annihilation of self in republican fraternity and mutual support.

Visions of the Daughters of Albion

As I have said, it is clear at the outset of *Visions* that Oothoon is a contrary of Thel in character. By the end it is also clear that the poem itself is a contrary of *The Book of Thel* in form. The stately minuet of *Thel* is shaken, to be sure, by the shrill final movement, but that disruption is slight compared with the ballooning of what might have been a brief episode in *Visions,* a climactic speech by Oothoon, into a huge and static coda. The tersely narrated episodes of the first two plates are so heavily outweighed by this coda that they dwindle in retrospect to a mere introduction to it, or a setting of the stage for it, like the brief actions of an opera that set off the arias. Blake seems impatient to get to the dialogues and especially to Oothoon's magnificent, long and unanswered speech that occupies half the poem. We might take as an expression of that impatience the very brevity of the sketch of the Thel-like situation that Oothoon starts out from, as if, once we see that Oothoon and Thel are sisters, we are meant to feel Oothoon's eagerness to leave the vales of Har behind.

The 'Argument' begins

> I loved Theotormon
> And I was not ashamed[.]

Blake seems to jump the gun here and present Oothoon's striking difference from Thel, out of sequence, before he catches himself and remembers that she and Thel were once alike.

> I trembled in my virgin fears
> And I hid in Leutha's vale!

As they stand these lines are puzzling, for it is hard to imagine why she trembled and hid, if not out of shame. She soon enough plucks up her courage, however, and the rest of the 'Argument' is in the right order even though it breaks off before the act of regeneration that marks her as Thel's opposite.

> I plucked Leutha's flower,
> And I rose up from the vale;
> But the terrible thunders tore
> My virgin mantle in twain.

When we meet Oothoon in the poem proper she is wandering woefully in her vales just as Thel did, 'seeking flowers to comfort her' (plate 1, line 4). The Marygold she meets preaches the same lesson that the Lilly taught Thel, but by responding so differently to it Oothoon enters an entirely different world. Oothoon is so brave and generous and so wonderful an orator that she seems to occupy an entirely different plane from Thel's. Yet Oothoon's fate is no less a disaster, and the long complaint that fills two-thirds of the poem sounds a little like the voice from Thel's grave plot. Thel's shriek corresponds formally to Oothoon's wail (plate 8, line 11), and both poems conclude in stasis and repetition.

It took Thel three dialogues before she brought herself to step out of her vales, whereas Oothoon is ready to soar at the first prompting. She does not differentiate herself from the Marygold as Thel did from the Lilly (and the other creatures); Oothoon sees that she is a Marygold herself, that she both is and has a flower. When she picks it she shows that she shares the Marygold's faith in the eternal replenishing of generously given flowers. She shows the pluck or heart that will be so characteristic of her – what Blake elsewhere calls 'The undaunted courage of a Virgin Mind' (Penguin edition, page 158, line 6). She is about to offer her virgin flower to her lover, of course, but by placing the glowing Marygold between her breasts she is not decorously disguising a lower intention but announcing that the frangibility of the hymen, the 'little curtain of flesh' that Thel laments, is of no moment to a glowing heart. Even if the flower is plucked by one she does not love, it may be restored by one she does love, if he shares her heart and vision.

The Marygold resembles Thel's Lilly as an emblem of love and self-sacrifice, but it is not explicitly a part of an ecology of 'use' like all the creatures of Har; it stands for one thing, its own renewal after voluntary sacrifice, 'because the soul of sweet delight / Can never pass away' (plate 1, lines 9–10). But why a marigold? Like the sunflower, which Blake honours in 'Ah! Sun-Flower' (*Songs of Experience*), the marigold is notably heliotropic (its Latin name is *solsequium*). When Oothoon turns her face to where her 'whole soul seeks' (plate 1, line 13), she turns heliotropically eastwards to her dawning love (with a pun, perhaps, on her flower's Latin name). Thomas Carew relies on the 'amourous' marigold's proverbial love of the sun for the main conceit of his poem 'Boldness in Love', and indeed the failure of the bashful morn to win the flower with his 'sighing blasts and weeping rain' calls to mind Theotormon's behaviour over a different sort of failure. According to Erasmus Darwin, for whose poem *The Botanic Garden* Blake engraved some plates, the marigold even imitates the sun in giving off a faint flash or spark. A sufficient reason for the presence of the Marygold in this poem, however, is one all English gardeners would know: its hardiness and regenerative power. It blooms from early spring to late autumn and is known to survive frequent beheadings and early frosts.

Having plucked the Marygold, Oothoon flies delightedly 'over Theotormon's reign', or realm, presumably to find Theotormon himself, but she is suddenly 'rent' or raped by Bromion, who then gloats over his possession to Theotormon, calls her a harlot and gives her to him to marry. Instead of taking vengeance against Bromion, as we might expect, Theotormon goes to pieces and can do nothing but weep in jealousy. Oothoon undertakes a purifying ritual with eagles in order to unite with Theotormon, but it does no good. The rest of the poem is given to speeches: first a set of three, in which each character expresses his or her position in this triangle, and then a long unanswered oration by Oothoon. The three-part exchange is in only the most formal sense a discussion, and when it yields to Oothoon, whose prophetic rhetoric seems less to originate in her than to pass through her from a deeper source, her spirit dominates the poem. The 'visions of the Daughters of Albion' are Oothoon's visions, and their power is so great that the poem barely makes a pretence at containing them; it is Blake speaking through Oothoon. By the same token, she is a figure of the poet, whose language and vision are superior to those around her – superior, but powerless. She remains trapped. Bromion says no more because he hardly needs to; his act has permanently stamped Theotormon's outlook even while the woman he raped has shrugged it off. Theotormon, for whose soul the other two contend, falls silent because he has nothing to say. Oothoon keeps up her wonderful, inexhaustible talk, but it seems to bring her and her sisters no closer to freedom.

It is likely that *Visions of the Daughters of Albion* was inspired in part by Mary Wollstonecraft's *A Vindication of the Rights of Woman*, published in early 1792, for Oothoon can be seen as the radicalized spirit of Wollstonecraft herself. Blake knew her, and even illustrated one of her books, a set of stories for children. Perhaps the 'Daughters of Albion' are the intended readers of *A Vindication,* who will adopt her vision and shed at least their internal chains. Wollstonecraft also addresses men, however, as Oothoon addresses Theotormon, for both know that women cannot liberate themselves alone. Theotormon, deaf to Oothoon's appeals, might then represent the reactionary male response to Wollstonecraft's book, and by putting that audience into his own book, Blake may be appealing over Theotormon's head to enlightened male readers on Wollstonecraft's behalf. Oothoon is none the less a much more radical and liberated soul than Wollstonecraft, who disparaged love, despised sensations and considered this life to be a preparation for the next. Blake was later to 'rehabilitate' John Milton by bringing him back from heaven and removing his false religious garments; he may be doing the same to the still living Mary Wollstonecraft through the free and naked spirit of Oothoon.

For Oothoon's powers of regeneration, generosity and forgiveness of injury are breathtaking. After howling and writhing after her rape (but not weeping over it like Theotormon), she calls on 'Theotormons Eagles' to

> Rend away this defiled bosom that I may reflect.
> The image of Theotormon on my pure transparent breast.

> (plate 2, lines 15–16)

Whatever else this may mean, and it is far from obvious why Theotormon should have eagles at all, it certainly brings about Oothoon's inward purification, the restoration of her virginity through her love for Theotormon. Perhaps, like Christ, she is willingly doing penance for other men's evils, or perhaps, like Prometheus suffering under the eagle of Zeus, she is resisting tyranny for the sake of her ideals. The eagles in any case seem to re-enact her rape, so that when they are finished she bears not the stamp of Bromion but the image of Theotormon. It is, alas, an ideal image, for it no longer corresponds to the real Theotormon, who cannot see that she is unchanged, or even sweeter than she was (see plate 3, lines 17–19). When he smiles at the sight of the eagles rending her, he smiles 'severely', as if he thinks that she deserves this second ordeal; when she reflects the smile, we must believe, she does not reflect the severity. It is as if she not only regenerates herself but the man she loves, in her mind at least, showing him, if he would but look at her, that she sees him as better than he is.

Oothoon's two great speeches, moreover, are the most eloquent and moving manifesto of free love, of 'the heaven of generous love' (plate 7, line 29), in all of Blake's writings. She appeals to Theotormon to arise and greet the new dawn of love; she denounces religion and abstract morality, which are only subtle elaborations of sexual possessiveness; she paints a lurid picture of the miseries of loveless marriage, where 'she who burns with youth ... is bound / In spells of law to one she loathes' (plate 5, lines 21–2); she celebrates 'Innocence! honest, open, seeking / The vigorous joys of morning light; open to virgin bliss' (plate 6, lines 5–6); and she even offers to catch girls and 'view their wanton play / In lovely copulation bliss on bliss with Theotormon' (plate 7, lines 25–6). It is for the sake of this wonderful oration, I think, that the events of the story, told in sometimes baffling brevity, exist at all, and they reward the reader's struggle through the first two plates.

A shift occurs early in the first of Oothoon's two long speeches, however, that should again give pause to the reader, if he or she is not swept onwards by the surging rhetoric. Her appeal to Theotormon to arise and enjoy the dawn that has arrived for his enjoying suddenly yields to what then becomes the main theme of all the remaining speeches: the question of what we can know, or the relation between 'sense' and 'thought'.

> Arise my Theotormon I am pure.
> Because the night is gone that clos'd me in its deadly black.
> They told me that the night & day were all that I could see;
> They told me that I had five senses to inclose me up.
> And they inclos'd my infinite brain into a narrow circle.
> And sunk my heart into the Abyss, a red round globe hot burning
> Till all from life I was obliterated and erased.

> (plate 2, lines 28–34)

With 'They told me' there is an awkward but arresting change in topic. We have seen no 'they', no instructors, and indeed no moment during the rapid movement of events in which Oothoon could have been instructed. Except one, perhaps: the rape itself. As Yeats was to ask about another rape in 'Leda and the Swan', 'Did she put on his knowledge with his power?' She may have briefly put on the Bromionic view of things, as she howls and writhes and considers herself defiled, but then she summons her own deeper knowledge and power to discard it and return to Theotormon. What is strongly suggested here is that her rape by Bromion and what 'they told' her are the same thing.

This equation may be easier to accept if we take Oothoon to be thought itself, or free thought, and see her story as her growth into spiritual liberty. In the same way that Thel in one of her aspects is an emblem of the 'fair eyed' dew, Oothoon starts out as a sigh. She both sighs for her absent lover and she represents the collective sigh of the enslaved Daughters of Albion. When she rises up from the vale, she suggests the cry or prayer of the oppressed appealing to heaven. From a sigh or prayer she turns into a breeze, a zephyr or, indeed, a strong west wind blowing from the land of liberty, as 'Over the waves she went in wing'd exulting swift delight' (plate 1, line 14) to her lover. Later she cries, 'Love! Love! Love! happy happy Love! free as the mountain wind!' (plate 7, line 16), her spirit still free even while she is bound in some sense to Theotormon.

What happens to this breeze, somewhere over the Atlantic, is that it meets a contrary wind, a thunderstorm named Bromion (which is Greek for 'roarer' or 'thunderer'). There may be an allusion here to Ovid's story of the rape of Oreithyia ('mountain wind') by Boreas the North Wind, though the names more closely echo those of a tale by Ossian. Bromion's thunder, in any case, overcomes Oothoon's spirit, but only for a moment – for, as the 'faint maid' lies on his bed, 'soon her woes appalld his thunders hoarse' (plate 1, line 17). Something in her faint cries drains his thunders of their loudness; the blackening stormcloud is struck pale or faint himself by the cry of the oppressed, just as the chimney sweeper's cry 'appalls' the church in 'London'. Though Bromion has wind enough to vaunt over her, and shakes the 'cavern with his lamentation' in a speech a little later (plate 4), her spirit is stronger than his, and he will soon be forgotten. It will be Oothoon's voice, filled with the spirit of love and prophecy, that fills the rest of the poem.

Theotormon once worries over what we might call the essence of Oothoon: 'Where goest thou O thought! to what remote land is thy flight?' (plate 4, line 8). His own thoughts are rock-bound, or cave-bound, as are Bromion's, unable to transcend their material or sensory environment. When Bromion announces that the swarthy slaves are 'Stampt with my signet' (plate 1, line 21), he hints at an epistemological meaning beyond that of commercial branding. The imagery of imprinting and impressing, of waxen tablets and sealing-wax and seals stamped with a signet, inevitably suggests John Locke's doctrine of the *tabula rasa* or blank slate of the mind and the impressions left on it by 'sense', the only source of knowledge that he recognized. The Lockean doctrine, in other words, justifies rape – the rape of a blank or virgin 'slate' by presumptuous sensory intruders, the rape of a little child by the world of 'facts' impressed into its memory. When Oothoon complains that 'they told' her that she has only five senses, she bears a double grievance, for she has been raped both by the doctrine itself, which tells her she is only an impressionable creature of instruction, and by its imposition on her at the hands of her instructors.

In eighteenth-century England Locke's doctrine of sensation was the prevailing theory about the acquisition of knowledge, and Blake attacked it in his very first experiments with copperplate engraving, *There is No Natural Religion* (in two series) and *All Religions are One*. It is with Oothoon, however, that Blake first finds his true voice of prophetic indignation at the mental constriction of his countrymen by this miserable philosophy of passivity and worldly instruction. Oothoon's diatribe against Lockeanism becomes an exhibit in her own case, for she pours out from an inner fountain a torrent of knowledge that she could not possibly have learned from experience.

Those who are stamped by such instruction, she says, are 'inclos'd' in a narrow circle, and their five senses are not so much the inlets of knowledge through that circle as they are the circumference of the circle itself. The island cave that Oothoon and Theotormon inhabit is the inside of Theotormon's rocky skull circumscribed by the teachings that he has accepted as his own. Oothoon, as a free thought or spirit, would like to fly to a remote land, with Theotormon, as she once flew to him, but he will not let her. His grave thoughts are too heavy for flight; he remains petrified. He has been brought to believe in the substantiality of thought – 'Tell me what is a thought?' he asks, '& of what substance is it made?' (plate 3, line 23) – and in the spatial and temporal location of everything that exists. He asks where, he asks when, and he distrusts news of remote places, including, no doubt, the good news of liberty from Oothoon's homeland. He prefers the comforting familiarity of 'the present moment of affliction' (plate 4, line 9) to the supposititious gospel of forgiveness and renewal that Oothoon preaches and (invisibly to him) practises. He fails to recognize that 'the thoughts of man, that have been hid of old' (plate 3, line 13) are innate within him, like the inborn senses and 'joys' of the various species of animals that Oothoon recites (plate 3, lines 2–13; plate 5, line 33 to plate 6, line 1). Man's thoughts, joys and sorrows are not to be found in a garden or in a river or on a mountain, just as wisdom in the Book of Job cannot be found in the 'depth' or in the sea or in the 'land of the living', nor can it be weighed for the price of gold (Job 28). The answer to Theotormon's anguished questions is 'Here' and 'Now'; he need only arise and embrace her, making her spirit his own.

He does not do so, and the poem ends unhappily. Or rather the poem simply stops, without really ending, for we are told that 'Thus every morning wails Oothoon', while Theotormon sits 'conversing with shadows dire'. Modern liberated readers might wonder why such a strong and spirited girl feels bound to stay with such a weak and spiritless boy. Why doesn't she fly off once again to a worthier lover? Mary Wollstonecraft uses the common Lockean terminology to discuss how difficult it is for one to transcend the habitual associations laid down in youth: 'So ductile is the understanding, and yet so stubborn, that the associations which depend on adventitious circumstances, during the period that the body takes to arrive at maturity, can seldom be disentangled by reason.' Women, lacking the opportunities men have to exercise their reason, are damaged more than men by 'this habitual slavery, to first impressions' (*A Vindication of the Rights of Woman*, chapter VI). Oothoon has disentangled herself at a stroke from the adventitious circumstances that were supposed to enclose her, but she remains somehow chained to the boy who first impressed her.

There is evidence from elsewhere in Blake's writings that he felt that women were incomplete without a loving relationship to men (and vice versa), and that women, or at least the female dimension of any human mind, were secondary though complementary to men, or the male dimension. He probably took for granted that the liberation of women (via liberal divorce laws, education, the right to vote, and so on) was impossible without the active collaboration of men, so in her representative function Oothoon can only petition the men to stop treating women as property. The political or allegorical level of the poem, which demands that the poem come to a halt without a resolution, is itself complicated by the distinct suggestion that Oothoon also represents Negro slavery, the movement for the abolition of the slave-trade having reached a peak, and failed, just before Blake wrote *Visions*. Bromion might then be seen to represent the slave-owners, as well as their spokesmen in Parliament (such as Edmund Burke), who had recently out-stormed the liberal abolitionists (symbolized by Theotormon). The slaves are not going to free themselves. Oothoon also represents 'the soft soul of America', as we have noted (see plate 1, line 3), but America was not only the land of liberty but the land of slavery; Bromion, who claims that 'Thy soft American plains are mine' and who has stamped as his own 'the swarthy children of the sun' (plate 1, lines 20 and 21), would then seem to be an *American* landlord and slave-owner, unless we are to think of him as a British landlord about to be ousted by the American revolutionaries. It is difficult to sort out all these levels. In his longer poems Blake has a way of launching symbols and then forgetting to look after them properly, though I should add that good Blake readers learn that it is usually they who have failed to look after them properly. In this poem Blake seems to have made the themes of sexual possession and the nature of knowledge central, as if they somehow underlie the other issues. Perhaps they do. He returns, in any case, to the political level in *America: A Prophecy,* which puts the War of Independence at the centre but manages also to embrace an emblematic rape, women's liberation, the theory of knowledge and cosmic events on a grand scale.

America: A Prophecy

This brief epic encapsulates the events of the American Revolution
from the early 1770s to the British defeat in 1781, with a 'prophecy'
that looks ahead twelve years to the resurgence of revolution in France
in 1793, the year Blake finished the poem. It begins, however, with a
difficult 'Preludium' set in another dimension from most of the action
in the main poem. This is about a boy named Orc, a nameless 'shadowy
daughter' of an even more shadowy Urthona and the cosmic consequences of Orc's 'fierce embrace' of the daughter. We seem to enter
upon a vast and already taken-for-granted mythological context for
the political and military events shortly to be told; the characters are
not introduced or described, any more than Achilles is when we first
meet him in the *Iliad*. There is no great harm if readers skip the
Preludium at first and go straight to the main poem – there Orc
reappears, though he is introduced as if for the first time – but they
should eventually come to grips with it. The kind of criss-crossing of
symbolic levels that complicates *Visions* recurs here with a vengeance,
and whether or not it is crucial to understanding the rest of *America*, it
is the kind of thing that Blake does repeatedly in his later and longer
visionary poems.

> The shadowy daughter of Urthona stood before red Orc.
> When fourteen suns had faintly journey'd o'er his dark abode;
> His food she brought in iron baskets, his drinks in cups of iron;
> Crown'd with a helmet & dark hair the nameless female stood;
> A quiver with its burning stores, a bow like that of night,
> When pestilence is shot from heaven; no other arms she need:
> Invulnerable tho' naked, save where clouds roll round her loins,
> Their awful folds in the dark air; silent she stood as night;
> For never from her iron tongue could voice or sound arise;
> But dumb till that dread day when Orc assay'd his fierce embrace.

'Red Orc' certainly suggests a hellish figure, as the name recalls Orcus,
one of Virgil's and Milton's words for hell. But, as Blake makes clear in
The Marriage of Heaven and Hell, the devils are the forces of energy
and desire, confined in subterranean hells by the 'angelic' forces of
reason and repression. This reversal of the devil–angel polarity continues throughout *America* and engenders a number of amusing ironies.
Here in the Preludium, however, everything sounds very serious and
portentous, as if we are in a gothic novel, with a plot from the old
romance tradition of enchanted maidens and captive knights. Urthona
is never identified. (In *Europe: A Prophecy* Urthona is a male figure

75

whose lapse seems to bring about a repressive era; in later works he is the spirit of imagination whose earthly counterpart, Los, resembles Blake himself.) We might imagine him a kind of evil wizard 'stern abhorr'd' (line 11) as Orc says, who has bound his daughter in spells, for she is dumb until the 'dread day', 'long foretold', when Orc embraces her. But she is not exactly a Sleeping Beauty awaiting her prince: she is his gaoler who brings him his iron rations in iron baskets and cups, and she is armed with helmet, bow and quiver full of pestilential arrows. She seems to be a cross between Miranda, who brings food to Ferdinand, chained by the wizard Prospero in Shakespeare's *The Tempest,* and a Greek goddess, Athena or Artemis, virgin warrior or huntress. (Orc, meanwhile, seems to be a cross between Ferdinand and Caliban, not to mention Ariel with his soaring spirit.)

But it gets stranger yet, and the romance elements seem to yield to mythology or allegory. The daughter is

> Invulnerable tho' naked, save where clouds roll round her loins,
> Their awful folds in the dark air; silent she stood as night[.]

Her silence seems at one with the darkness that enwraps both her and Orc, as if this 'iron' age is also the dark age before the sun of enlightenment and revolution disperses it. As we shall see, there is a great deal of emphasis in the main poem on sight, on eyes, on vision; here in the Preludium Orc strains to see her nakedness: 'my red eyes seek to behold thy face' but 'In vain! these clouds roll to & fro, & hide thee from my sight' (lines 19–20). She somewhat resembles the spirit of Liberty, celebrated by many poets in Blake's time as a virgin courted by English heroes, now herself enslaved and only dimly perceived until an American youth, or youthful America, embraces her. But her role as bringer of food, the stress on her loins, the sexual act that follows, and especially the speech she finally makes about 'my American plains' suggest that she is America herself, the virgin land, still under the possession of the English absentee landlord Urthona (perhaps a pun on 'earth-owner'), and mainly unknown and uncultivated until the colonists seize her for their own.

Orc, as the spirit of the American colonies, seems to complete a term of years and then assert his independence. No very good explanation has been found for the 'fourteen suns' that have to pass, but they may suggest that Orc has achieved his sexual maturity if not the age of reason. When he finally takes the daughter, in what certainly looks like a rape, her womb 'joys' (conceives?) and she smiles her first smile. The clouds enveloping her now part so that not only can he see her but she can see him, and when she does see him, her very first speech (plate 2, lines 7–17) begins with a cry of recognition: 'I know thee, I have found thee, & I will not let thee go'. (Albion's Angel will also recognize Orc, but as someone rather different.) It seems to 'dawn' on her that this is her destined saviour and proper mate, even though his fiery embrace causes her to feel howling pains – labour pains, presumably, as she gives birth to revolutionary Sons of Liberty. What she recognizes in Orc goes beyond the spirit of the colonists, however, for she says,

> Thou art the image of God who dwells in darkness of Africa;
> And thou art fall'n to give me life in regions of dark death.

(lines 8–9)

This force that has emerged from the depths seems to be a fallen angel, perhaps even Jesus himself, descending from the heights to bring life to the realm of death. He also 'dwells in darkness of Africa', not America. If 'Africa' is meant to suggest Egypt, as elsewhere in Blake's work it probably does, then we are reminded of the enslavement of the Hebrews and their Exodus from it, which in Christian terms is a foreshadowing of the salvation of sinners from regions of dark death by Christ. But if this is meant to suggest Negro slavery in America, recalling the 'swarthy children of the sun' whom Bromion owns in Oothoon's America, then we have a disturbing reminder that the Sons of Liberty did not liberate many slaves. Blake may have hoped that they would – that the Revolution would set all races and both sexes free – but as it is only here that he touches on the Negro question, we have to assume that he is not differentiating groups among the revolutionary Americans.

The Preludium ends abruptly with the daughter's maiden speech – the Voice of America, perhaps, now heard around the world – except for four lines that Blake may have added a year or two later and then omitted from nearly all copies. These lines tell us that the Bard who has just sung the Preludium has shattered his harp in despair; perhaps Blake felt desperate over the war between England and France, or over the grim events in France itself. In most copies, then, we go abruptly from the mating of Orc and the female to the confrontation between Britain and America. Most of the remainder of the poem stays on a more earthly plane, however symbolically presented, but what we might call the 'preludic' level intervenes from time to time in somewhat the same way as the supernal gods in the *Iliad* keep watch over mortal doings and sometimes take part in them. Orc reappears; there is a host of angels and 'Guardians'; the lost continent of Atlantis is mentioned;

some mysterious astronomy concerning Mars gets a few lines; and near the end Orc's highest opponent, Urizen, dramatically intrudes.

The plot is fairly simple. The confrontation between the Americans and the Guardian Prince of Albion, who glare at each other across the Atlantic, escalates to the point where a 'Wonder' arises over the Atlantic – 'a Human fire fierce glowing' (plate 4, line 8) – who seems to embody the unified spirit of revolution or the desire for liberation. This frightens Albion's Angel Prince, who recognizes the 'Wonder' as Orc, whom he calls the Antichrist and arch-rebel, now arisen from the hell where he had been confined. Orc agrees with this characterization up to a point – in plate 8 he describes how he stamps the Ten Commandments to dust and 'scatter[s] religion abroad / To the four winds as a torn book' (lines 5–6) – but he is really the spirit of 'fiery joy' and the 'soul of sweet delight' (lines 9 and 14). Orc's speech incites Albion's Angel to call on the thirteen angels (or spirits) of the colonies to sound the alarm and repress this spirit of rebellion. But instead the thirteen angels hold a meeting, debate the question and then defect to the American side. At the same time, the thirteen colonial governors grovel at the feet of Washington and the British soldiers throw down their arms in fear.

Albion then commands vast plagues, like new armies, to blight the land, but the Americans all 'rush together' in one united spirit of self-defence. The plagues recoil onto Albion's Angel and the other authorities of England, and cause disunity in London, Bristol and the inner empire of Ireland, Scotland and Wales. New spirits of desire and liberty arise in England itself. But Albion has one last trick. Urizen, symbolizing the principle of repressive law, pours down a misty blizzard that blocks the sight of Orc and his bright fires; the authorities reassume control – but only for twelve more years, when Orc will reappear just across the Channel in France.

The most dramatic moment, and the turning point of the plot, is the refusal of the thirteen angels of the colonies to respond to Albion's call to arms. For twenty-seven lines, filling a whole plate (number 9), the Angel gnashes his teeth over the 'terrible men', Washington, Paine and Warren, who face him on the opposite shore, and bewails the terrible rebirth of rebellion personified in Orc, who faces him in the sky. Four times he shouts, 'Sound! sound! my loud war-trumpets & alarm my thirteen Angels!' But nothing happens.

> No trumpets answer; no reply of clarions or of fifes,
> Silent the Colonies remain and refuse the loud alarm.
> (plate 10, lines 3–4)

The scene then quietly shifts to, of all places, Atlantis, 'those vast shady hills between America & Albions shore; / Now barr'd out by the Atlantic Sea', where there is a palace, the 'archetype of mighty Emperies' (plate 10, lines 5–6, 8). It is here that the thirteen angels meet to discuss the loud demands from Albion. Atlantis must represent something like the original union or empire of humankind, before it was drowned in the Flood. By holding their council within this 'archetype', Blake is suggesting, the angels are invoking the original principles of human brotherhood: it is not they but Albion's Angel who is sowing division.

Boston's Angel, of course, is their leader, and his fiery speech raises issues not yet discussed by either Orc or George Washington (but which Oothoon dwells on in *Visions*). What god or angel, he asks, gave orders 'To keep the gen'rous from experience till the ungenerous / Are unrestraind performers of the energies of nature' (plate 11, lines 8–9)? 'Generous' here seems to mean not only 'giving' and 'liberal' but also 'generative' or 'fertile'. The ungenerous or miserly earth-owners have kept from the land those who should work it and manage its resources. We should remember that 'colonist' comes from the Latin *colonus*, meaning 'farmer'. After reading the *Songs of Experience* we might wonder why Boston's Angel finds it outrageous that the generous should be kept from 'experience', but the word here may have something of its older sense of 'fulfilment in practice', rather than any negative associations. Those who are young and strong should till the land, and own it, whereas Albion's decrees have sent them to 'the sandy desart' (line 11) instead. We touch here upon the symbolic meaning of Orc's 'generous' impregnation of the shadowy daughter. To claim independence from Britain and to claim ownership of the land are the same act.

Boston's Angel concludes his speech with a *non serviam* like Lucifer's: 'no more I follow, no more obedience pay' (line 15). He and the other twelve angels then tear off their robes and throw down their sceptres. They do not wait for the loyal angels to expel them – there is no war in heaven – but willingly quit their stations and, in language that echoes *Paradise Lost,* 'indignant they descended / Headlong from out their heav'nly heights' (plate 12, lines 4–5). They take their stand beside Washington, Paine and Warren. Blake writes in *The Marriage of Heaven and Hell* that he reads the Bible in its 'infernal' sense, finding deep rebellious truths beneath the orthodox angelic overlay. He reads *Paradise Lost* in the infernal sense as well, and even claims that Milton was 'of the Devils party without knowing it' (plate 5). By likening the defecting colonial spirits to the rebel angels of Milton, Blake not only parodies the royalist view of the American Revolution but slyly suggests that the rebellion in heaven was entirely justified. *America: A Prophecy* is in many ways a recasting of *Paradise Lost,* with more than a hint that it was not lost at all, or not for long: it has been regained in America.

We may translate this crucial shift in the balance of power in mundane terms as the transformation of public opinion in the thirteen colonies from loyalty to Britain to loyalty to each other. Blake stresses that the success of the movement for independence depended on the co-operation of all the colonies; the breaking of one union was the forging of another. When the enraged Albion sends his vast host, 'Arm'd with diseases of the earth' (plate 13, line 15), to blight America, what saves America is 'the fierce rushing of th'inhabitants together' (plate 14, line 12). There is a kind of general strike, or at any rate a halt to business as usual, in New York, Boston, Pennsylvania and Virginia. And

> Then had America been lost, o'erwhelm'd by the Atlantic,
> And Earth had lost another portion of the infinite,
> But all rush together in the night in wrath and raging fire
> The red fires rag'd! the plagues recoil'd! then rolld they back with fury
> On Albions Angels . . .

(plate 14, line 17, to plate 15, line 1)

The uniting of the Americans makes the plagues recoil on the heads of those who sent them, and on the spirits of London, Bristol and York, together with those of Ireland, Scotland and Wales. These plagues, then, seem to mean more than the scourge of war, more even than actual destruction of crops that war often brings: they seem to signify disunity itself. War is certainly the deepest kind of disunity, and when Albion's Prince tries to keep his empire together by violent means, he is hoist with his own petard: disunity spreads in his own kingdom. Blake may be alluding to the parliamentary opposition to the war and to the disaffection of many English subjects, especially those in the port cities that traded with the colonies. He is also suggesting the revolutionary ferment spreading (by 1793, at least) in the original empire of England, the never fully subjugated Celtic fringe. It is as if he is glancing ironically at the very names of the two countries: to be reluctant subjects under a United Kingdom is a false unity now rightly threatened by the free and voluntary 'rushing together' of the United States.

The influence of the United States on the inner empire of England may be the hidden meaning of the most enigmatic passage of *America*, the one depicting Mars (plate 5).

> Albions Angel stood beside the Stone of night, and saw
> The terror like a comet, or more like the planet red
> That once inclos'd the terrible wandering comets in its sphere.
> Then Mars thou wast our center, & the planets three flew round
> Thy crimson disk; so e'er the Sun was rent from thy red sphere;

The *ad hoc* character of this passage – there is nothing further about Mars in *America* and no other astronomy so strange in all of Blake's work – tempts the reader to root out a source, but diligent hunters have turned up nothing approaching it so far. When Mars (Ares) first appears in literature (*Iliad* 4.439–41), he comes with three satellite companions, Fear, Terror and Strife, but they are all warriors, not planets or comets. As for comets in general, Albion's Angel has good reason to feel terror before them, for he knows (having read Shakespeare) that 'Comets, importing change of times and states', have presaged the doom of some of his predecessors: when 'meteors fright the fixed stars of heaven ... These signs forerun the death or fall of kings' (*1 Henry VI*, 1.1.2; *Richard II*, 2.4.9–15). He sees comets as planets that have become unmoored from their orbits around a 'disk' or from the sphere that 'inclos'd them; 'planet' means 'wanderer' (from the Greek *planetes*), after all, as if it is in the nature of planets to become comets unless they are controlled by a 'center'. He regards Orc first as one of these comets that has wandered out of orbit, and then sees that it is worse than that: the 'terror' resembles the original central planet itself, and the Angel is terrified that the three planets now orbiting around it will be drawn into Orc's sphere. Orc, in other words, has become a rival to Albion's Angel and is competing on equal terms for the 'planets three'. And what are they? They must be 'Ireland and Scotland and Wales', now infected with the disease of revolution (an astronomical term itself) and drawn to the new centre of gravity in the west.

Such political astronomy was common enough in Blake's day, as the star-spangled banner of the United States reminds us, but Blake may well have read a 1780 pamphlet by Thomas Pownell, Member of Parliament and former Royal Governor of Massachusetts, which made interesting use of this symbolism in an argument for American independence. In the 1760s Pownell had argued that the colonies must remain disunited and that 'Great Britain ... must be the centre of attraction to which these colonies ... must tend. They will remain under the constant influence of the attraction of this center ... in their respective orbs.' In his new pamphlet Pownell changed sides (like Boston's Angel) but maintained his astronomical imagery. The United States, he wrote, is a 'new primary planet' which would 'have effect on the orbit of every other planet, and shift the common center of gravity of the whole system of the European world'.

We are still left wondering why Blake singles out Mars. Surely the sun would make a better centre for planets to revolve around? But in this story (and it seems to be the narrator now, not the Angel, who speaks), 'the Sun was rent from thy red sphere'. As astronomy this is preposterous, but as political symbolism it should now be clear enough. Orc is not really a comet or even Mars; he only looks that way to the dim-sighted Angel. He is really the sun, now rising in the west; he will draw all the planets, including Mars, into his sphere of influence. It is Albion's Angel who is Mars, the Roman god of war, not Orc. It is the Angel Prince who has inherited the Mars-based Roman Empire; it is he who 'burns in his nightly tent' (plate 3, line 1) at the outset of the poem, rising at midnight and sending flaming red meteors round the land. The revolution in America is also what Thomas Paine terms a *'counter-revolution'* (*Rights of Man,* Part Two): 'Government founded on a *moral theory, on a system of universal peace, on the indefeasible hereditary Rights of Man,* is now revolving from west to east, by a stronger impulse than the government of the sword revolved from east to west.' When the sun rises, when 'The morning comes, the night decays, the watchmen leave their stations', then the Angel of sword-government will be eclipsed, at least in America. 'The Sun has left his blackness', or redness, '& has found a fresher morning' (plate 6, lines 1, 13).

But it is so far only in America that this new dawn has arisen. Amid the redounding plagues the fires of Orc also lick across the ocean, and inspire new desires for freedom in Albion's realm. As the guardians and priests turn into reptiles, revealing their true nature, and hide from the fires of Orc, suddenly 'The doors of marriage are open' and the females are 'naked and glowing with the lusts of youth' (plate 15, lines 19, 22).

> For the female spirits of the dead pining in bonds of religion;
> Run from their fetters reddening, & in long drawn arches sitting:
> They feel the nerves of youth renew, and desires of ancient times,
> Over their pale limbs as a vine when the tender grape appears[.]

> (plate 15, lines 23–6)

This reminds us of Oothoon's vision of free love, as well as Orc's boast that he stamps religion, and 'pale religious letchery' (plate 8, line 10), to dust, so that sexual delight can be expressed. Blake may be alluding to a bill passed by the House of Commons in 1781 that removed the priests from the marriage business: all that was required for marriage was civil registration. But the House of Lords threw it out, and slammed shut the 'doors of marriage' again.

And so it is that Urizen, who was named and addressed by Oothoon but did not appear in *Visions*, now steps in to quash the glowing ardour of the young Britons. As the shadowy female in the Preludium had said to Orc that 'thy fire & my frost / mingle in howling pains' (plate 2, lines 15–16), Urizen fights fire with frost: 'His stored snows he poured forth, and his icy magazines / He open'd on the deep' (plate 16, lines 9–10). This sounds like a blizzard of reactionary propaganda and repressive laws, and it has not only a chilling effect on acts of freedom but a blinding effect on free thought. For Urizen's bleak weather is capable of 'Hiding the Demon red with clouds & cold mists from the earth' (line 13), concealing him from the sight of Albion's people. Then, combining the door image with that of blinding, Blake concludes by reporting how all the European powers close the 'five gates' of the senses, preserving their ancient religious laws against the besieging fires of Orc, which will burn around them for twelve more years before France succumbs.

To appreciate fully the turn towards the five senses at the end, we should go back to the beginning again and note the importance of sight and vision throughout the poem. While still chained in his cavern, Orc strains to see the shadowy daughter: 'my red eyes seek to behold thy face / In vain: these clouds roll to & fro, & hide thee from my sight' (plate 1, lines 19–20). After their sexual union she shows herself to him, and sees him herself, for the first time. Meanwhile, down on America's shore, the first thing Washington says to his compatriots is 'look': look at the threats from Albion, and at the heavy chain that binds us across the sea. That 'look' causes Albion in dragon form to 'Appear to the Americans' (plate 4, line 1), and their reaction to the apparition causes the 'Zenith' to display itself as a 'Wonder' in the form of Orc. Then 'The King of England looking westward trembles at the vision' (line 12). When Albion's Angel finally speaks to Orc he asks, 'Why dost thou come to Angels eyes in this terrific form?' (plate 7, line 7). Phrases such as 'I see' and 'in sight of Albions Guardian' keep recurring. Though it is an auditory effect that marks the turning point – the silence following Albion's noisy alarm – it is the 'visions of Orc' that propel the story forward.

The struggle between America and Albion, then, is mainly a contest of visions: each side stages extravagant spectacles to impress the other, or induces the other to project its own extravagant fears and fancies, while making declarations and remonstrances of its point of view or way of seeing things. It is, as Blake sees it, much more an ideological war than a military war, a battle for the hearts and minds of the Anglo-American people. Americans are the stronger in this war, for their visions are visions of truth. As Thomas Paine wrote in *Rights of Man,* Part Two, 'such is the irresistible nature of truth, that all it asks, and all it wants, is the liberty of appearing. The sun needs no inscription to distinguish him from darkness; and no sooner did the American governments display themselves to the world, than despotism felt a shock, and man began to contemplate redress.' Albion's Angel admits that 'clouds obscure my aged sight' (plate 9, line 12), and his soldiers seek somewhere 'to hide / From the grim flames; and from the visions of Orc' (plate 13, lines 8–9). Only the cold obfuscations of Urizen stave off the ardent visions, and then only temporarily.

Blake was perfectly aware that the American War of Independence was quite bloody, that Saratoga and Yorktown were as much a part of it as pamphlets and propaganda. His list of seven patriots at the opening includes four military commanders alongside Franklin, Paine and Hancock, and he calls them all 'warlike men'. The rushing of the inhabitants together is described as 'fierce', and there is much rage and fury throughout. The plagues that Albion's Angel sends are certainly violent and destructive. Nevertheless it is not on 'corporeal war', as he later called it, that Blake dwells. The only time that 'British soldiers' are mentioned they throw down their swords and muskets and hide from Orc. The main American weapon, Orc and his flames, cannot refer to the Minute Men or the Continental Army, for the flames spread to England and threaten to set afire all of Europe. It is mainly a spiritual war, the 'Spirit of '76' against, let us say, the lords spiritual of England. That is why Blake invokes Milton's war in heaven and the Book of Revelation, both of which are spiritual wars conceived in a very literal way. The visions that each side sees are all revelations, and when Urizen sends his clouds and mists he in effect concedes that England has no power of vision left, and can only cling to the 'ancient heavens', now torn by newly independent planets.

The Designs

It is not surprising that a poem so concerned with a contest of imaginations should be accompanied by spectacular illuminations. The designs of *America* are among the most brilliant and interesting that Blake ever engraved. Most of them, however, are difficult to interpret. A picture may be worth a thousand words, but it cannot do everything that words can do. Without the control of a text which it 'illustrates', and without iconographic conventions of the sort we see at work in medieval and Renaissance art, a picture may show us something but may not easily assert the truth of something or deny it, exhort us to do something, or posit the likelihood that something will come about. Blake's designs seem at best only partly governed by such texts or conventions. The difference between an indicative assertion and a counter-factual subjunctive, easy to manage in language, may be beyond picturing. Freud wrote that 'No' seems not to exist in dreams, and the same may be true in pictures. Yet there is a counter-factual passage in the text of *America* that affects one of the designs over whose interpretation critics have not agreed.

> Then had America been lost, o'erwhelm'd by the Atlantic,
> And Earth had lost another portion of the infinite,
> But all rush together in the night in wrath and raging fire
> The red fires rag'd! the plagues recoil'd . . .

(plate 14, lines 17–20)

The design in question is on the previous plate (13). At the top, ocean waters have flooded up to the legs of an apparently dead woman, naked and about to be torn apart by an eagle or vulture; below the text a naked man lies on the ocean floor about to be eaten by several fish and serpents. By itself we might take the design to be 'indicative' of the horrors of war, like the title-page (plate i): it suggests the completeness of the slaughter in its male and female prey and in its predators of the air and water, while it recalls two of the fates most dreaded by the warriors of the *Iliad* – carrion for birds and carrion for fish. The dead might be Americans, or, given that the eagle and serpent are both symbols for Orc in the Preludium, we might take the scene as being the Guardian Prince's vision of Orc's devastation, of Britons as well as Americans. As the sea is so prominent, however, we cannot ignore the line about the Atlantic on the next plate, and in its context that line transforms the design from the indicative to the subjunctive mode. This is what *would* have happened had the colonists *not* rushed together. When we read that they did, we are the more thankful for this successful act of fraternity, having vividly seen in advance the consequences of failure.

The uncertain mode of this plate is typical of the others, some of which might also be counter-factual or hypothetical, without a verbal passage telling us that they are. In the beautiful plate 7, two children are asleep with a ram, lying under a graceful willow-tree on which birds of paradise are perched. Is this a false paradise like the vales of Har in *Thel,* or is it a glimpse of the real paradise in the past or future tense? There are children mentioned in the middle line of the brief text, the ones whom Albion's Angel claims are about to be devoured by the 'serpent-form'd' Orc. Is this, then, the Angel's vision of the Garden of Eden, or the heaven of Enitharmon (named here), about to be destroyed by the serpent? Who owns this image?

In plate 11 a young man rides a swan through the sky and three children sit astride an enormous but apparently tame serpent, as they do at the conclusion of *Thel.* No such scene is described in the text, but we might take the design as the 'Orcian' contrary to the Angel's view of the serpent at the gate of heaven. Far from devouring the children while they sleep, he wakes them up and offers them a wonderful ride. It is also counter-factual like the design on plate 13. Boston's Angel, who may be the man seated aloft on the swan, like Apollo, asks in his resignation speech why the 'generous' tremble.

> who commanded this? what God? what Angel!
> To keep the gen'rous from experience till the ungenerous
> Are unrestrained performers of the energies of nature[.]

(lines 7–9)

We might interpret the swan and the serpent as the energies of nature and their riders as the generous ones who are not allowed to 'perform', or not yet. Boston's Angel thus creates a prophetic hypothetical space, filled by the design, where the generous may find their experience, free of the commands of abstinence.

The competition of visions that makes up so much of the action of *America* extends to the designs: they bid us ask who sees them – the Americans, Albion's Angel or an omniscient observer – and in what tense and mode. Plate 4 prompts us explicitly to ask such questions, as if to train us for the more contestable plates that follow, for the two parts of its design are placed below isolated lines that serve as captions, the first and last lines of the text: 'Appear to the Americans upon the cloudy night' and 'The King of England looking westward trembles at the vision'. What appears to the Americans is the Prince in 'dragon form' (plate 3, line 15), and there he is at the top of the design. Next to him, almost as if fleeing from him, is a downward-diving king in human form, which the Americans do not see, although they may devoutly wish they did. Is it an omniscient reader's view, prophetic of the fall twelve years hence? Or is it the king's view of himself, weakened already, 'trembling' over the revolution? Trembling at something else, perhaps a beached sea-monster (an orc?) but more likely a fallen tree, is a male tearing his hair, kneeling near another male who looks up at the basilisk and king and shelters a child. The lower 'caption' implies that at least one of the men is the king in human form, horrified at the damage done to his ancient oaks by the revolutionary westerlies. Yet the second man and the child inspire sympathy, so we may wonder if this lower group does not represent the Americans, who see not a prophetic royal fall but a king swooping upon them, bringing a hurricane of war and famine. It may be that the two 'captions' should switch positions.

The next plate (5) also seems to present falling kings or angels – three of them – cast into hell through a serpentine orc-screw by what looks like a revolutionary tribunal of three tribunes with scales and a flaming sword. We know, however, that Blake disliked 'justice', which in his view was only rationalized revenge, and the flaming swords that keep us from the Edens of imaginative desire. Blake probably wept few tears at the execution of Louis XVI, however, and may have taken on the role of Daniel, who tells another king that he is weighed in the balances and found wanting. Is this design the handwriting on the wall for kings to read? Jesus warns us to judge not, that we be not judged, but Paul advises Christians differently: 'Know ye not that we shall judge angels?' (I Corinthians 6:3).

This double perspective suggests another reading, one which absorbs the outlook of Albion's Angel into the Orcian one and which corresponds closely to the text about Mars. It is Albion's Angel who sees or remembers what the text describes: the emergence of a new centre, a sun, from the old sphere of Mars. Orc and his three comets or planets are Mars-like to the Angel, but they have in fact left behind the martian or martial sphere to find a 'fresher morning' free of war and imperialism. What *we* see are the three planets, now in orbit around Orc, casting off their former selves, their old Adams, into the pit. They have weighed themselves and found themselves wanting, or wandering, and now they are leaving their erroneous portions behind, to be enclosed in the sphere of the serpent. In Albion's sight, of course, they are now wandering from their proper orbit around himself and heading for trouble with Orc, but Albion cannot tell which end is up, or whose end has come.

All this is highly speculative, but we cannot miss in the physiques of all six figures, and especially in the contorted postures of those who are falling, an allusion to Michelangelo's *Last Judgement*. It is Albion's Angel who will insist that Armageddon is at hand, but the Americans, forced into acting out this script, will manage to reverse the roles. In his draft commentary on his own *Vision of the Last Judgment* (1810), Blake says that 'whenever any Individual Rejects Error & Embraces Truth a Last Judgment passes on that Individual' (E 562). This idea, of a piece with Blake's usual interiorization of orthodox theology, encourages us to interpret the six figures as three former angels – the 'Guardians of Ireland and Scotland and Wales', now defecting like the thirteen angels of the colonies – and their three wandering former selves. It also suggests that the main question is not the passing of a sentence from outside upon Albion's Angel, in the person of King George III, for the fate of this one historical human being is no more important than that of any other. As a part of all our minds, a projection into the heavens of one of our own spiritual powers, Albion's Angel embodies our own responsibility and our own error. To wrestle with all the texts and designs of this demanding work, Blake seems to say, is to wrestle with error in ourselves, especially the error of gravitating around the sphere of priesthood, tyranny and war.

5. *The Marriage of Heaven and Hell*

Between 1790 and 1793, while he was engaged with *Songs of Experience*, *Visions* and *America*, Blake also wrote and engraved his one great prose work, *The Marriage of Heaven and Hell*. Not surprisingly, it is unlike anything anyone has written before or since, although scholars have tried to name its genre and find precedents for it, and despite its strangeness it has become, after the joint *Songs*, the most popular of Blake's works. Its 'Proverbs of Hell', perhaps the greatest collection of invented proverbs in English, have appeared on many walls and placards as well as in books, and most of the rest of the work shares something of their pithy wit and radical surprise. It contains some of Blake's most forthright declarations of his basic beliefs (or so they seem) and his most oblique satire on the beliefs he rejects. It is also his funniest book.

But what is it exactly? It has been called a 'Menippean satire' in the tradition of Petronius, Rabelais, Swift and Voltaire: a loosely organized prose work, sometimes with verse interludes, that uses caricature, extravagant fantasies and invective to ridicule social follies. Its more directly visionary parts, and even its invective, recall Isaiah and Ezekiel (who appear on plates 12 and 13), so it has been considered a 'prophecy' no less than *America* or Blake's other 'prophetic' works. Because one can trace an intermittent personal narrative about what 'I' saw or did, the book has also been taken as a miniature *Künstlerroman*, a story about the education of a poet-prophet.

Its form is about as heterogeneous as one could imagine, though certain abstract patterns are visible. It begins and ends with verse, while the main body is all prose; the two 'poems' are none the less quite prosaic and not much like one another. There are five sections entitled 'A Memorable Fancy', and these accounts of imaginative experiences alternate with more detached reflections or historical surveys. If one adds the opening of plate 3, about the 'new heaven' and 'Eternal Hell', and 'The Voice of the Devil' on plate 4, one can come up with seven visions followed by seven commentaries, which might suggest that Blake modelled his book on the Book of Revelation with its nested sevenfold patterns. The experience of reading *The Marriage*, however, and of viewing the designs, is rather one of great variety and unpredictability, as if it is essential to *our* education as a poet-prophet that we be ready to learn from anything and everything that comes along. The structure of the book has been called 'dialectic', and certainly one of its *subjects* is the struggle and reconciliation of opposites, but there is nothing in it so orderly as an unfolding progression of arguments or Hegelian antitheses.

Arguments with Swedenborg and Milton

The structureless structure of *The Marriage of Heaven and Hell* is partly determined by the main target of its satire, the writings of Emanuel Swedenborg. Swedenborg has few readers today outside the small Swedenborgian churches that still exist in Britain, America and Europe, and Blake's many readers are understandably reluctant to drop their Blake and pick up Swedenborg in order to get the point of the send-up. *The Marriage* can be appreciated and enjoyed with no knowledge of Swedenborg besides what Blake himself provides, but its intended audience seems to have been members, or ex-members, of the Swedenborgian 'New Church', and even non-Swedenborgian readers in Blake's day were much more likely to have recognized him and taken him seriously than readers are today.

He should not be underestimated. Goethe spoke well of him, Coleridge called him a great mind, Emerson made him one of his 'Representative Men', and Balzac has one of his characters say that 'his religion is the only one a superior mind can accept'. Many other superior minds found him attractive and interesting. A Swedish metallurgist and mining engineer, member of the Swedish parliament, linguist, inventor, polymath, Emanuel Swedenborg (1688–1772) experienced religious revelations and wrote voluminous theological works, many in the form of biblical commentaries, such as *Apocalypse Explained* (in six volumes) and *Arcana Caelestia* (in twelve). He interpreted the Bible in its 'internal' sense (which Blake puns upon when he speaks in plate 24 of its 'infernal' sense), revealing the 'arcana' hidden in its literal or historical sense. If we have the key to reading them, the historical events of the Old Testament thus become allegories of our spiritual condition, offering complete guidance in our religious and moral lives. Swedenborg maintained that the key is contained in the 'science of correspondences', according to which everything outward and visible has an inward and spiritual cause, and for every perceived thing or event there is a spiritual counterpart, even for such objects as trees, mountains, thistles and snakes.

Knowing no more than this, we can surmise that Blake would be interested, and indeed he and Catherine attended the first General Conference of the New Jerusalem Church in London in April 1789, and subscribed to the forty-two propositons that the assembly put forward, including such assertions as 'All are redeemed' and statements against slavery. Copies of three works by Swedenborg, with Blake's often sympathetic annotations, have come down to us, including *Heaven and Hell,* the most immediate inspiration for his riposte. Within a year he was through with the New Church: as we shall see, it is easy to deduce on plate 3 that 1790 was the date of his departure. Just what caused his change of mind remains doubtful, but the events in France three months after the General Conference found a different response in him from that of the majority of his fellow Swedenborgians, who were at pains to make known their political passivity and loyalty to the king. A dispute over the right of 'concubinage', the right that Swedenborg himself seems to have affirmed – that of taking a sexual partner outside marriage if the marriage were spiritually dead (if one's partner, for example, did not join the New Church) – led the majority to expel the pro-concubinage party and suppress all references to the issue in the church minutes. It is easy to guess which side Blake took in this schism, and the very word 'marriage' in his title may echo the importance he placed on the debate about it. Even without this backsliding of the New Church into moral and political orthodoxy, Blake was bound to tire of Swedenborg and his tedious biblical commentaries. But we must take *The Marriage of Heaven and Hell* as an intervention in a sectarian debate as well as a proclamation of universal truth.

The title-page implies that the book will be filled with marriages, as six or eight naked couples embrace while flying upwards through hell's flames to the surface of the earth, on which there are two more couples. The words 'HEAVEN and HELL' are placed below ground level, as if to say that heaven is really part of hell. But we must wait for the third plate to find stated explicitly the reversal of angel and devil that undergirds the whole book.

'The Argument' of plate 2, though there is nothing obviously satirical or witty about it, may signal that we are indeed reading a satire, since 'arguments' are usually prose summaries of verse narratives (as in *Paradise Lost*), and this one is just the opposite. It is also harder to understand than most of what it purports to summarize. In any case it tells a parabolic story in which 'the just man', whose righteousness brought life out of the desert, is usurped by 'the villain' and driven back into it. The just man seems to correspond closely to 'Rintrah', a character Blake introduces here as a frame for the poem and then drops

91

for the rest of *The Marriage*: he is the voice roaring in the wilderness, an outcast prophet, perhaps the voice of the true Swedenborgianism angry at the hypocrites of the New Church, but certainly 'the voice of honest indignation' described by Isaiah (plate 12). Indeed, it might be said that Rintrah and the just man have an 'argument' with the villains who have displaced them.

> Once meek, and in a perilous path,
> The just man kept his course along
> The vale of death.
> Roses are planted where thorns grow.
> And on the barren heath
> Sing the honey bees.

(plate 2, lines 3–8)

'Once' seems to modify 'meek' and thus set up a contrast to 'now', when the just man rages, but it may have the sense of 'once upon a time' and thus modify the whole clause, like the temporal adverbs that begin each of the other three stanzas – once, then, till, now – clearly marking four stages of the story. The second half of the first stanza switches to the present tense, however, as if to contrast 'once' with 'now' from the start. But these lines may also be taken as a vivid historical present and not a departure from sequence; they would then be recapitulated in the next line, 'Then the perilous path was planted'. If we take them in this sense, we are given a richly interesting question to ponder: what is the connection between what the just man does and the blooming of the heath? The poem pointedly avoids saying that the just man planted the roses by using the agentless passive (twice), as if God planted them, or as if they planted themselves, as an effect of the just man's keeping to his path through the vale of death.

'Vale of death' is, of course, this life, like 'the valley of the shadow of death' (Psalm 23) in the common interpretation, and we may think of Christian in *Pilgrim's Progress* who walks through this same valley on a perilous knife-edge path. In plate 3 Blake tells us to look up Isaiah 34 and 35, and when we do we find contrasting scenes, one where the Lord in indignation devastates Edom, filling it with thorns and wild beasts of the desert, and the other (Zion) where 'The wilderness and the solitary place shall be glad for them [those who live justly]; and the desert shall rejoice, and blossom as the rose' (35:1). 'The Argument' shares Isaiah's linking of living justly with blooming deserts, but the vengeance of the Lord is put off to the end, where the raging of the just man and the roaring of Rintrah, not to mention the 'hungry clouds', portend a day of reckoning.

The just man, meanwhile, seems to bring about a complete transformation of death into life, even a reversal of the Fall of Man (lines 9–13).

> Then the perilous path was planted:
> And a river, and a spring
> On every cliff and tomb;
> And on the bleached bones
> Red clay brought forth.

Ezekiel in chapter 37 of that book tells of a valley of dry bones on which God lays flesh and sinew while the prophet promises a return to Zion from the land of death. 'Red clay', however, takes us back to Adam and the Hebrew word *adamah* signifying the 'red earth or clay' out of which Adam was made. A new Adam, a new beginning, has come about. But now we learn that there is another place, 'the paths of ease', where the villain has been watching and waiting (lines 14–16).

> Till the villain left the paths of ease,
> To walk in perilous paths, and drive
> The just man into barren climes.

We might think for a moment that the villain has chosen a perilous life, a life of spiritual justness and meekness, but of course the paths are no longer truly perilous, now that they are planted. Or, in a further irony, perhaps they are perilous to the villain but in a way that he cannot see since he thinks that he is expropriating desirable farmland from the one who has cleared and cultivated it. We remember the tirade of Boston's Angel in *America*, plate 11, against the dispossession of the generous and strong by the ungenerous rich. It is also hard to resist thinking of the history of Christianity in the radical Protestant version, according to which the original Church of Jesus and the disciples was infiltrated, usurped and corrupted by hypocritical priestly hierarchs, much like the story Blake tells in plate 11 of *The Marriage*.

The villain, in any case, is a serpent (lines 17–20).

> Now the sneaking serpent walks
> In mild humility.
> And the just man rages in the wilds
> Where lions roam.

Humility, the hypocritical counterpart of the original meekness of the

93

just man, masks the serpent who repeats what the first serpent did – drive out Adam and Eve to a land of thorns and thistles (Genesis 3:18). Has the just man learned anything? He no longer sounds very meek, rather more like the lions who share his wilderness. He must now know a 'sneaking serpent' when he sees one, even one who walks 'upright', as the serpent does in *Paradise Lost,* but will he return to his birthright? Or is he doomed to rage for ever?

Though Blake obviously identified himself with one of the *enragés,* and though during much of his later life he felt like an outcast prophet, in 1790 he is ready (see plate 3) to answer our questions with a vision of imminent reversal.

> As a new heaven is begun, and it is now thirty-three years since its advent: the Eternal Hell revives. And lo! Swedenborg is the Angel sitting at the tomb; his writings are the linen clothes folded up. Now is the dominion of Edom, & the return of Adam into Paradise; see Isaiah xxxiv & XXXV Chap:

This may be the most brilliant prose paragraph Blake ever wrote. It condenses his opinions about Swedenborg, his own mission, how to read the Bible and even the French Revolution into a few startling images, and once they are unpacked one can appreciate a witty cheekiness worthy of Swift at his best. Aside from the biblical allusions, there are two facts that this passage presumes we know. The first, which would have been known to Blake's apparent audience of Swedenborgians, is that Swedenborg, in *A Treatise Concerning the Last Judgment,* published in English only two years earlier (1788), declared that a 'new heaven' had been opened and that the Last Judgement had begun in 1757 in the spiritual realm. Thirty-three years was of course the age of Jesus at the time of the Resurrection: it is now 1790 and time for a new dispensation to 'rise up' and replace the one Swedenborg proclaimed. Swedenborg's writings (printed on linen paper, no doubt) cannot contain Jesus; he transcends them, casting them off like husks. Indeed they were the cerements that kept him decently dead, while now he is dangerously alive and active. (Blake may have been alluding to Milton's line in the *Areopagitica,* 'the ghost of a linen decency yet haunts us'.) And if Swedenborg is an angel (see Matthew 28:2–8), then Jesus must be – a devil! For 'the Eternal Hell revives'.

This is audacious enough, but a second fact, known only to Blake or his friends, makes it even more blasphemous and comic. Blake was born in 1757, when the 'new heaven' began, and is now thirty-three as he writes. He has just left the New Church, which was full of orthodox angels trying to suppress their sexual and spiritual energies, and he now proclaims a new age. Swedenborg is thus only an usher of the kingdom, a John the Baptist to – Blake himself! Whether Blake intended to found a new New Church we do not know, but he is taking a devilish pleasure in his send-up of Swedenborg's own solemn pretensions.

The 'dominion of Edom' is another reversal of usual expectations. Edom (also called Idumea), the land to the south of Judah, was settled by the descendants of Esau, who was cheated out of his birthright by the 'sneaking serpent' Jacob. Chapter 34 of Isaiah, which Blake cites, tells of the destruction of Edom, but chapter 63 speaks of the coming of the Lord *from* Edom, his clothing red with blood, to punish Zion, as if in fulfilment of Isaac's prophecy in Genesis 27:41 that Esau shall break the yoke of Jacob and 'have the dominion'. Esau, red and hairy (Genesis 25:25), is a prototype of Satan, as popularly conceived, and of Blake's Orc, while 'Edom' and 'Adam' are probably both derived from words for 'red'. It is not Israel or Zion that shall become the new Paradise, but Edom; it is not by angelic 'goodness' or 'mild humility' that England shall be transformed, but by their 'Contrary', 'Energy', which includes desire, honest indignation and faith in one's own vision.

Edom, finally, inescapably alludes to France, whose energetic self-liberation has frightened the good Swedenborgians – 'red France' (as Blake was to call it in *Europe*), the ancestral enemy to the south. In the fourth 'Memorable Fancy', the Angel conjures up a fearful vision of a monstrous serpent 'to the east, distant about three degrees' (plate 18), just the distance in longitude between London and Paris, though we might have expected Blake to have placed his map reference south or south-east.

After the brief parable in 'The Argument' and this even briefer apocalyptic vision, Blake now grants his readers a respite and forthrightly states his general convictions (plate 3).

> Without Contraries is no progression. Attraction and Repulsion, Reason and Energy, Love and Hate, are necessary to Human existence.
>
> From these contraries spring what the religious call Good & Evil. Good is the passive that obeys Reason[.] Evil is the active springing from Energy.
>
> Good is Heaven. Evil is Hell.

That nature and society are products of contrary forces is a commonplace going back at least to Heraclitus and Empedocles. Milton speaks of the 'struggle of contrarieties', in *The Reason of Church*

Government, as the way in which change comes about. The burden of the *Areopagitica* is that truth cannot flourish unless falsehood is free to do battle with it, an idea that comes closer to Blake's 'progression' than to the equilibria of the Greek philosophers. Swedenborg's contraries, too, were static. But two questions suggest themselves. First, does Blake believe that reality is 'dialectical'? Most Blake scholars are quite free with this term, but few of them bother to define it, leaving their readers to take it in the well-known Hegelian or Marxist senses. This is misleading. Blake's struggle of contraries, even if it is progressive, does not revolve through ever higher levels of comprehensiveness to a final synthesis, as proposed by Hegel and Marx. Even in Eternity, it seems, Blake imagines that there is continual struggle on a spiritual plane – 'Wars of mutual Benevolence Wars of Love', as he puts it near the finale of *Jerusalem* (plate 97, line 14). In this he is closer to Goethe's notions of polarity and *Steigerung,* the enhancement of identity through resistance and the growth of the spirit through widening but never-resolved spirals, than to Hegel's dialectic. When Faust is carried up to heaven, it is a reward not for his goodness but for his restless pursuit of truth and experience; in heaven he will continue his researches (and one imagines him having wonderful dialogues with Blake).

The second question is whether the two poles of the contraries are equal. They sound equal here – the title uses the word 'marriage', not 'dominion' or 'conversion', after all – but are we to believe that the just man, whose perilous way of life made the desert bloom, and the villain, who stole it from him, are moral or spiritual peers, or that Swedenborg is as necessary to human existence as Jesus or Blake? As we will see later, Blake's devils always get the last word, and in the end a particular angel has been converted altogether to the devils' party. Here in plate 3 Blake can sound detached and even-handed but, to adapt what he says of Milton (plate 5), Blake himself is of the devils' party without acknowledging it.

Blake's apparent stance above the fray has led some critics to warn us against taking plate 4, entitled 'The Voice of the Devil', as expressing Blake's own views. He is neither devil nor angel, they say, but the arranger of the 'dialectic' of the two. It is always good advice to distinguish author from character, as we had to do in reading the *Songs,* but here such warnings seem overly subtle and cautious. If some of the doctrines of hell sound excessive even for Blake, they are certainly infinitely closer to Blake than their opposites are. *The Marriage of Heaven and Hell* is not a marriage. It is a reversal of the war in heaven in *Paradise Lost,* a rout of the obedient angels.

In plate 4 the voice of the Devil tells us that dualism is an error, that the body is really 'a portion of Soul discernd by the five Senses' and that, far from being the source of evil, it is the origin of energy, life and eternal delight. The Devil is a monist, then, but not a materialist like Lucretius or (as some thought) John Locke. He more resembles the German idealists or 'phenomenologists' who take human perception as their starting point and derive the material world from it as a construct of sensation and thought. He is not far even from Swedenborg in this, but unlike the philosophers and theologians the Devil celebrates what we call the body as the 'only life', implying that soul (in the narrow sense) and reason are a kind of death. His most intriguing phrase may be 'the five Senses, the chief inlets of Soul in this age', for it implies in a casual gesture the enormous possibility that sometime in the past the soul had more senses than five, or more inlets than sensory ones, and may regain them sometime in the future. And indeed in plate 11 Blake asserts that the ancient poets had 'enlarged & numerous senses'. In that passage he goes on to tell how priests took over the poets' work and installed themselves over the common people. If we combine that story with the 'Voice of the Devil' passage, we see clearly the ideological uses of dualism, the politics of the mind–body split, for the Devil begins by declaring that 'All Bibles or sacred codes' have caused the dualist errors. Codes are drawn up by priests, and dualist religions serve dualist societies, the caste of the soul or reason governing the 'body' of the people.

For all his scorn of priests and presbyters, Milton supports the dualist view: that right reason must govern man's passions and that wise and prudent men must govern the realm. And Blake, for all his admiration of Milton, sees his orthodox and 'angelic' side clearly and now turns to confront it in one of the most extraordinary pieces of literary criticism ever written.

Coming to terms with John Milton was much more important to the fellow poet and republican William Blake than settling accounts with Emanuel Swedenborg. The latter task he more or less completes in *The Marriage*, while he pursues his conversation with Milton throughout his life. Here, in a work that celebrates the 'satanic' liberation of energy and desire, Blake must deal with the manifestly contrary message of the great revolutionary's major poem. Somehow Milton, or part of him, must be enlisted in the devil's forces.

Blake artfully begins his discussion (plate 5) with a general psychological proposition almost self-evidently true, taken in its own terms, but none the less threatening to orthodox moral teaching.

> Those who restrain desire, do so because theirs is weak enough to be restrained; and the restrainer or reason usurps its place & governs the unwilling.
>
> And being restrained it by degrees becomes passive till it is only the shadow of desire.

It must surely be the orthodox view that we restrain our desire not because it is weak but because it is strong and dangerous, and that we are able to do so because our reason, aided by faith, is stronger. Blake, as we saw, grants a role to reason, as the 'bound or outward circumference of Energy' (plate 4), but it seems quite secondary, not a true contrary, to desire. It has little strength in itself and can only accomplish its own desire for restraining and governing, if we can attribute desire to it, when it finds little resistance. The political metaphors used by Blake are common in the works of Milton and traditional moral theory from that of the Greeks onwards, but 'usurps' is well chosen and a bit of a shock, implying as it does that the place of desire is rightly higher than reason's, or at least equal to it. Reason, then, becomes a tyrant, whose continual domination over desire reduces it to a shadow of its former self. It is tempting to translate this little story into Freudian terms, but Freud's metaphors usually imply not a reduction of desire or libido under repression but a displacement of its energy; it never grows passive but only turns active elsewhere, perhaps in unhealthy directions. Something of this model can be found elsewhere in Blake – indeed why is the just man raging if he has grown passive after his usurpation, and what gives the 'Eternal Hell' the strength to revive? – but here Blake is altering this model a little to suit, rather startlingly, Milton's great poem.

> The history of this is written in Paradise Lost. & the Governor or Reason is call'd Messiah.
>
> And the original Archangel or possessor of the command of the heavenly host, is calld the Devil or Satan and his children are call'd Sin & Death[.]

Milton and his orthodox Christian readers might agree with Blake's allegorizing of the story – the Messiah (and the Father) as reason, Satan as desire – but stick at 'usurps'. That is Satan's view of Christ's elevation or 'begetting' (*Paradise Lost*, Book V, lines 603f.) and his revolt begins with his outrage at having to bow the knee to another superior. Blake ignores the fact that the Father has been the 'Governor or Reason' all along, and that Satan has willingly obeyed him, perhaps because Blake sees the Father as only 'Destiny' and not a true actor. This corresponds to Satan's own view that it was only in the 'fatal course' of things that he begot himself, owing nothing to a creator (Book V, lines 860–61). Milton calls the Son the Messiah when he takes command of the army of obedient angels and leads them to defeat the rebellious ones; the Messiah has thus dispossessed or usurped the 'original' commander.

We no sooner take in this rewriting of *Paradise Lost* than Blake throws in a rewriting of another work: 'But in the Book of Job Miltons Messiah is call'd Satan.' Satan in that work is one of 'the sons of God' who make proposals to God and carry out his commands – not a rebel but a prosecutor in the royal court. Satan has God's permission to torture innocent Job just as the Messiah at his Father's bidding inflicted unmerited torments on the unwilling angels. It is the same story, with the names reversed,

> For this history has been adopted by both parties
> It indeed appear'd to Reason as if Desire was cast out, but the Devils account is, that the Messiah fell. & formed a heaven of what he stole from the Abyss[.]

Book I of *Paradise Lost* shows the fallen angels, now in hell, building Pandemonium under the direction of Mulciber, who had been architect in heaven. The devils' account turns this dizzyingly upside down: the Messiah fell (upwards?) and constructed a heaven out of the energy he had found in hell.

Having glanced at Job we are now directed to the New Testament for evidence, presumably from the mouths of the orthodox, of this heretical claim.

> This is shewn in the Gospel, where he prays to the Father to send the comforter or Desire that Reason may have Ideas to build on, the Jehovah of the Bible being no other than he, who dwells in flaming fire. Know that after Christs death, he became Jehovah.

In John 14:16–18 Jesus tells his disciples, 'I will pray the Father, and he shall give you another Comforter, that he may abide with you for ever; / Even the Spirit of truth; . . . he dwelleth with you, and shall be in you.' This passage is one of the foundation texts for the doctrine of the Holy Ghost, the person of the Godhead most important for Blake but (as Blake goes on to say) least important for Milton. There is nothing in John, of course, or in Milton's version of the same passage (Book XII,

line 486), to warrant taking the 'Comforter' to be desire, but Blake
continues his psychological allegory and insists that the Holy Ghost,
the indwelling Jesus whom he elsewhere identifies with the imagination,
is the centre and source of all energy and creativity. Reason can only
compare and contrast and shunt ideas around, as John Locke showed;
the ideas that it works on must come from outside it, whether from
sensation, as Locke claimed, or from the fire of the inner light. He 'who
dwells in flaming fire', then, is not only the Devil but the Holy Ghost
(which appeared in tongues of flame at Pentecost) and Jehovah himself.
The Bible may confess as much when it depicts Jehovah appearing to
Moses in a burning bush. Christ, the Messiah who has been tormenting
mortals and angels after his 'fall', became the creative energetic Jehovah
after his death. We may not be wrong in taking 'death' here in the way
Blake often means it, as a psychological state of self-annihilation or
conversion, the sloughing off of the 'reasonable' Selfhood in favour of
the deeper imaginative spirit. That would make Christ an angel who
became a devil, like the one with which Blake concludes the last
'Memorable Fancy'.

In Blake's view Milton seems not to have understood any of this, at
least not consciously.

> But in Milton; the Father is Destiny, the Son, a Ratio of the
> five senses. & the Holy-ghost, Vacuum!
>
> Note. The reason Milton wrote in fetters when he wrote of
> Angels & God, and at liberty when of Devils & Hell, is because
> he was a true Poet and of the Devils party without knowing it[.]

Not many readers have warmed to Milton's God, who has been
called a monster of abstraction, much like Blake's Urizen, and whose
main function is to give lectures on predestination and foreknowledge.
Milton was not, strictly speaking, a predestinarian: 'if I foreknew,'
says God,

> Foreknowledge had no influence on their fault,
> Which had no less prov'd certain unforeknown.

> (Book III, lines 117–19)

But the distinction between making Man fall and making Man certain
to fall (though he was free not to) does little to rescue the moral
character of God, who seems less admirable even than Jupiter in the
Aeneid, who is mainly the voice of fate. Blake uses 'Ratio' as almost a
technical term, beginning with his two early sequences entitled 'There is
No Natural Religion'. It has something like its Latin sense of 'reason',

'basis' or 'ground', but with connotations of 'sum', 'product' or 'abstract result'. The Son, Blake seems to be claiming, is a product or creature of the sensory or bodily world, not its producer or creator. Are we to recall the Incarnation, when the Son assumed bodily form, or the sometimes ridiculous literalness of the war in heaven, in which the Messiah takes a leading part? He is not, in any case, the redemptive power in us that Blake elsewhere calls 'Jesus'. Nor does the Holy Ghost play that part in *Paradise Lost*. Milton was not a trinitarian, and gives little attention to the third person of the Trinity, though it is not quite fair to dub it 'Vacuum', if by this Blake means that it is entirely absent in Milton's poem. It does appear in the invocations that begin several of the books, just where in a poem it should appear, but it is not an effective agent in this destiny-burdened world.

Blake's 'Note' is justly famous, though most Milton scholars dislike it. The Note offers to explain the widely felt difference in poetic power between the descriptions of the fallen angels, especially in the first two books, and the much duller and drier accounts of God and the angels. It has also been widely agreed that there is a falling off of intensity in the last two books, where Adam is subjected to a history of the world in one long lecture. Consciously Milton shows how the devils grow more passive until they are only shadows of desire – they end by hissing like serpents – but Milton's own powers, according to this view, decline along with them, as if Milton were snuffing out his own energy and desire. In his *Defence of Poetry* (1821) Shelley argues similarly that 'Milton's poem contains within itself a philosophical refutation of that system of which, by a strange and natural antithesis, it has been a chief popular support. Nothing can exceed the energy and magnificence of the character of Satan as expressed in *Paradise Lost*.'

As this is a psychological theory, it would be fun to imagine what Blake would do if he were Milton's confessor or psychotherapist. 'The devil made me do it' no longer passes as an excuse, of course; Milton's confession would have to begin, 'My reason made me do it.' As it happens, Blake takes up Milton's greatness and his faults at length in *Milton* (begun in 1804), and one of the therapies he imposes on him is a struggle with the cold waters of reason. Though by then Blake abandons the 'satanism' of *The Marriage* and reverts to a more common usage of 'Satan' and 'Angel', Milton by the end of the poem becomes a liberated force of energy and desire, and a fit companion for the isolated and embattled William Blake. 'Milton!' Wordsworth wrote in a sonnet at about this time (1802), 'thou shouldst be living at this hour: / England

101

hath need of thee', but what England needs, in Blake's opinion, is not Milton's God or Messiah but exemplars of heroic rebellion like his fallen archangels.

Infernal Fancies

The first 'Memorable Fancy' tells of Blake's visit to hell, almost as a tourist collecting mementoes, and of his return to 'the abyss of the five senses' where most of us live in this age. He passes a devil writing with 'corroding fires', the very method Blake has used on the plates before us. He then shares with us his collection of seventy 'Proverbs of Hell'. Some of these are the best known and best loved of Blake's writings, and have had an afterlife independent of their context, but as a group they may represent an instalment of the 'Bible of Hell' (plate 24) which Blake promises at the end of *The Marriage*. A few of them are indeed reminiscent of the Book of Proverbs in the Old Testament, but most of them are quite different not only in purport but tone and form. Some of them pointedly reverse traditional proverbs. 'Tread on a worm and it will turn', for example, becomes 'The cut worm forgives the plow' (plate 7, line 11). That in turn belongs with 'Drive your cart and your plow over the bones of the dead' (line 7), which seems to arise from Jesus's command to 'Let the dead bury the dead' and his warning that 'No man, having put his hand to the plough, and looking back, is fit for the kingdom of God' (Luke 9:60–62). Jesus himself, then, Blake reminds us, had a devilish streak, and it would be an interesting exercise, while sorting the proverbs into common categories, to ask which ones might have been said by Jesus – not by Milton's Son, of course, but by the much more difficult and human individual of the Gospels.

Perhaps the most shocking and devilish of all the proverbs is 'Sooner murder an infant in its cradle than nurse unacted desires' (plate 10, line 7). That there might be something worse than murdering a baby startles us into attention. To 'nurse' infant desires without acting to realize them, Blake seems to say, is to torture before murdering. 'He who desires but acts not, breeds pestilence' (plate 7, line 10) belongs with this proverb, as does the story told in 'A Poison Tree' in *Experience*. Milton, by suppressing his desires (the devils), helped spread the pestilential religion of the angels of this world.

How did the angels gain control? Blake tells this story in plate 11, which has much in common with the Enlightenment critique of superstition.

The ancient Poets animated all sensible objects with Gods or Geniuses, calling them by names and adorning them with the properties of woods, rivers, mountains, lakes, cities, nations, and whatever their enlargd & numerous senses could percieve.

And particularly they studied the genius of each city & country. placing it under its mental deity.

All gods are human creations, 'mental' gods projected by poets such as Homer who had senses large and numerous enough to perceive things that we cannot perceive today. Lacking their faculties, we at least have their poems, which might help us to regain something of the lost visionary power, but the same 'usurpers' who frightened us into shrinking our senses still dominate our societies.

Till a system was formed, which some took advantage of & enslav'd the vulgar by attempting to realize or abstract the mental deities from their objects; thus began Priesthood.

Choosing forms of worship from poetic tales.

This second phase entailed an abstraction of the gods from the objects with which the poets had united them, the Zeus who was thunder on Mount Olympus becoming the Jupiter of the scales of destiny, supreme over gods and men, or the similar Jehovah of Mount Sinai becoming the heartless rationalist of *Paradise Lost*. Theological speculation then enters to systematize the poetic tropes and seal off any return to the original creative impulses behind them. 'Realize' is an interesting word, which strikes us at first as an unlikely synonym for 'abstract', but it means 'reify' here – to posit as real something that is only notional or that derives its significance from being inextricably bound to something else. This process was not initiated by disinterested philosophers but by ambitious would-be priests, for whom the truth of the system itself was less important than the forms of worship, which of course included sacrifices and tithes from worshippers. The newly reified gods were made active and superior beings who ratified the arrangements of their 'spokesmen'.

And at length they pronouncd that the Gods had orderd such things.

Thus men forgot that All deities reside in the human breast.

'All reification is a forgetting,' Theodor Adorno and Max Horkheimer have written (in *Dialect of Enlightenment*), and the paradigm of all reification is religion. Blake's mission in *The Marriage of Heaven and*

Hell and in all his other major works is to recall us to the state of being from which we have fallen, and which we can regain by shaking off the incrustations of false beliefs about God, gods or destiny.

Four 'Memorable Fancies' comprise the bulk of the remainder of the book. In plates 12 and 13 Blake begins his report of conversations with Isaiah and Ezekiel in a manner that is astoundingly matter-of-fact, parodying the Swedenborg who thought it the most ordinary thing in the world for an angel to carry him off somewhere: 'The Prophets Isaiah and Ezekiel dined with me, and I asked them...'. Blake at least has good questions to ask, and the answers are fascinating. His main concern is the same as that of the preceding plate – the degradation of poetic 'animation' into systems and forms of worship. If the prophets assert that God spoke to them, might they not be 'misunderstood, & so be the cause of imposition'? (At the end of the fourth 'Fancy' – plate 20 – Blake and an angel have 'imposed' their 'phantasies' on one another, whereas 'true Friendship' implies not imposition but 'opposition'.) In other words, to invoke God as sanction for one's prophecies, as all the prophets did, might cow one's listeners into belief, might impose a belief on them rather than inspire belief by precept or example. But Isaiah explains that he was in effect a pantheist poet. The God that he invoked was not perceivable by the senses: 'I saw no God. nor heard any, in a finite organical perception'. Instead his 'senses discover'd the infinite in every thing', and God spoke to him in so far as 'the voice of honest indignation is the voice of God'. That makes Isaiah quite a heretic by orthodox Old Testament standards – indeed a Blakean 'inner-light' devil.

Ezekiel explains the ancient Jews' intolerance of other gods by saying that the God they invoked was 'the Poetic Genius (as you now call it)', and that all other gods or principles derived from it. Blake was later to repeat Milton's assertion that the Greeks derived their arts and ideas from the Hebrews, but here his Ezekiel is making a somewhat different claim: all nations derive their gods from the original 'Poetic Genius', the human imagination, but it was the Hebrew prophets who said so in terms easily misconstrued by others. King David's fervent prayers only exacerbated the misunderstanding, as 'the vulgar came to think that all nations would at last be subject to the jews'. Like all 'firm perswasions', this one has come to pass, though not in the way it was anticipated, for Christianity and Islam, not to mention modern rationalist thought such as deism, have spread the Jewish God and moral code throughout the world. Ezekiel does not mention the role of priests in this process, but we may assume that they were the agents of insinuating and imposing the Jewish 'system'.

Blake concludes the dinner discussion by asking why both prophets did such outlandish things – Isaiah walking naked for three years, Ezekiel eating dung and lying on his side (see Isaiah 20 and Ezekiel 4). Ezekiel answers: 'the desire of raising other men into a perception of the infinite'. That is, only by provoking troubled questions, by opposing others' beliefs rather than by imposing one's own, can one shake them out of their presuppositions and return them to what Isaiah's senses discovered – 'the infinite in every thing', the origin of all poety and all belief.

If Blake on plate 11 and the two prophets on plates 12 and 13 have explained how the present state of things came about – priest-ridden, superstitious, moralistic, deferential to an imaginary God – Blake turns next to a prophecy of how things will be made right in the end. Fire, we are not surprised to hear, is the means of this consummation. We have been used to thinking of the fires of hell as destructive only, as a means of torture, but as part of his transvaluation of the Christian mythical universe, Blake rehabilitates these fires as pentecostal, creative and purifying. In this way, the 'cherub with his flaming sword', who has been barring the return of Adam and his progeny into Paradise ever since the Fall, will leave his post, whereupon the flames of his sword, as it were, will consume the 'whole creation'. But these flames will bring about its transfiguration: it will 'appear infinite. and holy whereas it now appears finite & corrupt' (plate 14).

What is really transfigured, obviously, is our own capacity to behold the creation. Our 'doors of perception' are to be purged. How will this come about? In plate 14 Blake makes two promises, both of them calculated shocks to the angelic temperament. The first is that 'This will come to pass by an improvement of sensual enjoyment.' No abstinence, chastity or other mortification of the flesh will open our doors to the universe; the mystical transports that some Christians have induced by these stringencies are false, narrow and diseased. We must expunge the notion that the body is merely the soul's temporary house or burden, which might be escaped or lightened by treating it with contempt. Following the voice of the Devil in plate 4, we must embrace the body as part of the soul and perceive it now not through the five senses only, by which it appears indeed as merely a physical thing, but rather grasp it through our cleansed perceptions as the source of infinite energy and delight. The second promise, I think, is that the cherub at Paradise will be Blake himself, for he will consume the false dualism by printing 'in the infernal method, by corrosives ... melting apparent surfaces away, and displaying the infinite which was hid'. Blake's method of printing becomes the root metaphor of his visionary programme, and his engraving tool becomes the flaming sword.

Having introduced himself as a printer and engraver, Blake turns in the third 'Memorable Fancy' (plate 15) to a 'Printing house in Hell' with six chambers. Four of them, at least, are occupied by beasts or beast-men, and we are invited to find allegorical meanings for them. This is not very easy to do. The dragon-man who clears away the rubbish might be the figure of 'sensual enjoyment' that Blake recommended to us in the last plate, who cleanses the perceptions of tradition's crust. The viper might be reason, or the 'Ratio' – past energy now at a standstill, congealed by other 'sneaking serpents' into beautiful religious icons (and books). The eagle and eagle-like men seem to be allies of the dragon-man, forces of energy and genius who expand our perceptions, so that the narrow chinks of our caverns widen to reveal infinite space. 'When thou seest an Eagle,' one of the Proverbs of Hell says, 'thou seest a portion of Genius. lift up thy head!' (plate 9, line 15). The design for this plate shows an eagle, its own head lifted up, clutching a long coiling viper, its head facing down. Raging lions in the fourth chamber remind us of Rintrah and the outcast just man; these melt metals into 'living fluids', to be taken by 'Unnam'd forms' in the fifth chamber and 'cast' (in a nice pun) into the expanse: you cast your type and then cast your bread upon the waters.

Whatever the allegorical meanings of these chambers, the striking thing about this vision is the bathos at the end, the let-down as we enter the final room: 'There they were reciev'd by Men who occupied the sixth chamber, and took the forms of books & were arranged in libraries.' All these mountainous labours have issued in a mouse of a library, where men have become books (just as we say 'Close thy Byron, open thy Goethe', – to echo Matthew Arnold – as if we had the authors themselves before us) and are then 'arranged' in alphabetical order: 'little coffins that are stacked on shelves', as Sartre wrote in *What is Literature?*, 'like urns in a columbarium'.

This tale is another version of *Paradise Lost* and of the usurpation of priests described in plate 11 – both are tales of the damping of poetic fires. Another version of this tale begins on plate 16: the antediluvian giants who formed this sensual world, and who sound like the ancient poets who animated all sensible objects, are now in chains, forged by 'the cunning of weak and tame minds' – those of the priests, vipers, angels or librarians of the world. Blake introduces new terms, 'Prolific' and 'Devourer', for the two classes. Two questions immediately suggest themselves. First, why do we need the Devourers at all? Are they not mere fetters on our creative energies? Here Blake makes clear that they are necessary: 'the Prolific would cease to be Prolific unless the Devourer as a sea recieved the excess of his delights'. This does not seem to be quite the same polarity as that of reason and energy, where reason is the bound or outward circumference of energy. It is tempting to think of the Devourers as consumers, as readers and buyers of books, without which indeed the Prolific would cease to publish, but that thought seems to flatten Blake's suggestive imagery. He may be trying too hard to be fair, and to provide evidence for the 'marriage' in his title, even though he has given us no concrete cases of equal partnership between any pair of contraries.

The second question Blake himself anticipates: 'Some will say, Is not God alone the Prolific? I answer, God only Acts & Is, in existing beings or Men.' The angelic Swedenborg had denounced this idea as an 'execrable heresy', and a heresy it certainly is. It might be called 'Holy Ghost Unitarianism', the reduction of the Trinity to the third person instead of the first; some have called it atheism. It even has a whiff of pantheism, if we take 'existing beings' seriously. It brings us back to the original 'ancient' state where the poets were in imaginative contact with all objects and knew that all deities reside in the human breast.

If he insists on their interdependence, Blake does not believe that the two classes can be 'reconciled'. They should remain enemies or contraries, and the attempt to reconcile them is 'religion', which destroys 'existence'. Almost everywhere in Blake the word 'religion' is pejorative, as if its etymological sense of 'binding' (the same root as 'ligament') were its central meaning. Jesus, he continues, did not found a religion. As our Shepherd, he did not fold us all into one congregation, but separated the sheep from the goats, and he brought not peace but a (no doubt flaming) sword. Religion is an invention of the priests, and it is only a 'Negation', in Blake's later terminology, not a 'Contrary'.

As if he has just read this execrable heresy, an angel rushes into Blake's next 'Memorable Fancy' (plates 17–20) to save him from himself. You are heading straight for hell, he warns. Undaunted, Blake suggests that they take turns showing each other their eternal lots. The Angel leads Blake through a series of allegorical stages like the chambers in the printing house – stable, church, church vault, mill, cave and void – which resembles a radical history of Christianity presented from its humble birthplace in a stable, through prosperous worldly institutions and analytical theologies that grind the original spiritual intuitions into dust, to the vacuous darkness of today. As the two of them hang over an immense 'nether sky' – the Angel's notion of hell – the Angel himself is suspended in a fungus, a parasite like the priestly caterpillar of one of the 'Proverbs of Hell', which hung head downwards, like a bat, perhaps, who cannot tell up from down. Eventually they see spiders flying or swimming through the air, as Swedenborg said that they would in his book *Wisdom of Angels*: they represent 'infernal love' and their webs are their lusts. Blake's lot is pinpointed between the black and white spiders, as a fitting punishment for his love of contrariness, but no sooner is the place indicated to him when cloud and fire burst out from it, and then a 'monstrous serpent' appears in the east, an Orc-Leviathan like the one that the Prince of Albion fancies he sees in *America,* standing for everything that the Angel hates and fears.

The frightened Angel leaves Blake alone to his fate, but the vision disappears as soon as the Angel stops 'imposing' it upon Blake, and Blake finds himself 'sitting on a pleasant bank beside a river by moon light hearing a harper who sung to the harp'. The harper sings another proverb of hell: 'The man who never alters his opinion is like standing water, & breeds reptiles of the mind.'

It is now Blake's turn to show the Angel his lot, but the journey that they take together is less a projection or imposition of Blake's 'metaphysics' than a parody of the Angel's. They fly westwards, as if towards America, but then leave the earth and plunge into the sun. This presumably purges them of the traces of smoke and fungus, and Blake emerges dressed in white. But instead of the Book of Life, which we might expect, Blake carries Swedenborg's volumes, which are so heavy and so remote from true illumination that he sinks all the way out to the remotest verge of the solar system, the sphere of Saturn. Blake's companion, the 'saturnine' Angel, belongs here, or just beyond it, in the 'void. between saturn & the fixed stars'. Just beyond the 'fixed stars', traditionally, is the empyrean or heaven, but the Angel, who confidently expects to end up here, will fall one stage short. There may be a little joke in this as well, for in 1781 the planet Uranus, then called 'King George's Star', had been discovered by Sir William Herschel, and Blake may be suggesting that the loyal Swedenborgians who shuddered at the French Revolution have followed the star of England's king, whose light is invisible to the naked eye. Gravity, in any case, seems reversed, for Blake and the Angel, ballasted by Swedenborg, 'sink' out of the sun. The angel's lot is to be at the bottom of the solar system, the furthest from the sun's light and heat.

Then Blake and the Angel see the stable and church again, and this time Blake opens the Bible at the altar and plunges in, driving the Angel before him. He seems to have opened the Bible at the Book of Revelation, for they see seven houses of brick, which must be the seven churches that John addresses from Patmos. Entering one of them, they observe the most grotesque and disgusting of the visions, like one of Dante's scenes of hell: monkeys (who can only imitate or 'ape' each other) fight, couple and devour one another as if they are Christian sects or biblical commentators who have turned the one true Church into a zoo or battlefield. The stench drives them both into the mill, where Blake finds one more volume, a 'skeleton' that he recognizes as Aristotle's *Analytics,* which Swedenborg had praised. Blake holds it up as the final reduction to absurdity of Swedenborg and the final revelation of the Angel. It all comes to this: the 'mills' of logic producing not a single original idea. As he says in the next plate (21), Swedenborg's writings are 'only the Contents or Index of already publish'd books'.

This next section returns explicitly to Swedenborg and drops parody for 'plain facts'. It therefore requires little comment here. Having set up and brought down a straw man (his 'monkey'), Swedenborg imagined himself to be 'the single one on earth that ever broke a net' or escaped from the 'mind-forg'd manacles' of orthodox Christianity. He may have been wiser than the Church, but he was less wise, and far less original, than the alchemist Paracelsus (1493–1541) or the cabbalist Behmen (Böhme or Boehme, 1575–1624), and infinitely less original than Dante or Shakespeare (Milton goes unmentioned). The poet in Blake has now stated in forthright prose why he has abandoned Swedenborg and all his prosaic angels.

The fifth and final 'Memorable Fancy' (plates 22–4) returns to the heresy of plate 16. Here for the first time a devil directly disputes an angel, and it is no contest. There is no other God, says the 'Devil', than the gifts of genius in great men, and to honour those gifts is to worship God. The Angel, after turning various colours, denounces this opinion as idolatry, the worship of something other, and lesser, than the One God. The crux, as it were, is the nature of Jesus Christ. If, as the Angel claims, the One God is visible in Jesus Christ, then why may he not be visible in other human beings? In calling Jesus 'the greatest man', the Devil denies that Jesus was unique in kind. He has already denied that God is anything other than his visible gifts in great men; God is entirely immanent. The Angel and the Devil agree, however, in invoking Jesus as an authority on whether or not to obey the Ten Commandments, the Angel insisting that Jesus sanctioned them, the Devil citing Scripture for his purposes in a startling list of violations by Jesus himself. More fully presented in Blake's notebook poem 'The Everlasting Gospel', the Devil's Jesus is the antinomian version – found in Christian sects since ancient times and especially in seventeenth-century England – according to which Jesus came to 'fulfil' the law of the Old Testament (Matthew 5:17) by setting us free from it.

These citations overwhelm the Angel, who stretches out his arms to 'embrace' the 'flame of fire' – that is, the opinions of the 'Devil' – which consume his angelic portion and release him as Elijah, the prophet who rose to heaven in a chariot. In a final note Blake tells us that this converted Angel is now his 'particular friend' and fellow interpreter of the Bible in its 'infernal' sense, 'which the world shall have if they behave well'. The world not having behaved well, there is no sustained biblical commentary among Blake's writings, though it is not too much to say that most of his poetry is an implicit internal–infernal reading of the Bible. Blake may have found the form of an interpretation too straitened for his genius, too much like Swedenborg's ponderous volumes, and even self-defeating. What he did produce, at least in part, as he states in the 'Note', was 'The Bible of Hell: which the world shall have whether they will or no'. *The Book of Urizen* (Genesis), *The Book of Ahania* (Exodus) and *The Book of Los* (Genesis again) begin the new Blakean dispensation, and it is continued in sections of *Milton* and *Jerusalem*.

The Marriage of Heaven and Hell itself could be conceived as a marriage between both these latter projects. It gives us some wonderful 'infernal' readings of the Bible (and of Milton) and it presents itself as a 'new' New Testament, a Third Testament, which begins like the 'old' New Testament with the birth of a new age, the Eternal Hell. The conclusion of *The Marriage* proper (plate 24) states what may be Blake's most intense dislike in both 'old' Testaments in their orthodox reading, that they impose a law on us: 'One Law for the Lion & Ox is Oppression'. That line sits at the bottom of the plate as a caption to a drawing of mad King Nebuchadnezzar (of Daniel 4:33), the oppressor oppressed, who looks like a cross between a lion and an ox. To impose a common yoke on infinitely various human individuals is to reduce them to hybrids, to lowest common denominators of the 'Ratio'. What this book celebrates is the reciprocal opposition of combative free spirits, which is true marriage.

Probably engraved later than the rest of the book, the 'Song of Liberty' (plates 25–7) has a very different tone and symbolic register. It might be regarded as the first try at the 'Bible of Hell', but in any case it reads as a summary or first sketch of *America: A Prophecy*. It provides the first description of Orc, 'the new born fire' (number 8) and the first mention of Urthona by name. If the 'Argument' that opens the book restates the Fall of Man (i.e. Genesis), the 'Song of Liberty' that ends it restates Man's redemption (i.e. Revelation), for 'Empire is no more! and now the lion & wolf shall cease' (number 20). But this rather abstract symmetry and biblical parallel do not really 'contain' this heterogeneous section. It is as if world events had made Blake too impatient either to round out *The Marriage* formally or to wait for a new work in which to pour his new thoughts. But then, what better way to bring to an end a book that celebrates the road of excess?

6. From *Europe* to *Jerusalem*

If we were to continue discussing Blake's poetry and designs at the same level of detail, selective though we have been, this book would be ten times as long as it is. It is not only limitations of space, however, that bring us to a stop with *America* in 1793, before Blake began his 'Bible of Hell' with *The Book of Urizen, The Book of Ahania* and *The Book of Los*, and well before his major epics, *The Four Zoas, Milton* and *Jerusalem*. The best preparation for approaching these works is to read carefully the ones that we have discussed here, as well as *The French Revolution*, which we have somewhat arbitrarily left out.

When I first studied Blake seriously I also read a number of the most important critical commentaries, and their effect on me was not all to the good. They seemed so masterly and complete, so confident in their negotiations with the full range of Blake's symbolic system, that they made a beginner like me feel even more inadequate than I had already felt. They were like grand ocean liners steaming past a floundering swimmer, while what I needed was a raft, or a life-jacket, or even a few fellow swimmers to emulate. I hope the present book does not sound too certain or serene. I have tried to indicate doubts, difficulties and disagreements among interpreters, while encouraging the beginner with the idea that Blake, for the most part, makes rewarding sense. If any reader finds my own interpretations inaccessible or intimidating, he or she should keep in mind that some very good Blake scholars will disagree with most of them. The point is to get a little help at the outset and then dwell on the early poems until they seem credible and coherent. Then go on to the later poems, in the order that they were written. And then read some more criticism. (There is a short list of books about Blake following this chapter.)

Immediately after *America*, and a continuation of it, comes *Europe: A Prophecy* (1794), and it is famously difficult, mainly because of several dense, telegraphic narrative sections, a little like the early part of *Visions of the Daughters of Albion*. It is not even agreed which character speaks certain lines, and there are many new characters, several of them important. But Orc and the shadowy female return, and so does Albion's Guardian Angel and his habit of sounding the alarm. In the foreground are some real historical events, and there is also some satirical wit, exemplified in the passage about Newton blowing the

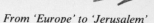

trumpet that the Angel could not blow (plate 13): the Angel wanted to awaken the dead to judgement but Newton, as if he is announcing his discovery of gravity, sends all the angelic hosts tumbling out of the skies to their graves.

Urizen, whom we have met as a cosmic ally of kings and priests, appears in *The Book of Urizen* (1794) as the 'primeval Priest' himself, but also as one of the 'Eternals' who make up the psyche of the 'Immortal', or unfallen Man. The Fall, according to Blake, takes place in a cascade of phases only the last of which is recognizably the Fall as depicted in Genesis or *Paradise Lost*. Blake's Bible begins before Genesis because it must explain, among other things, the origin of the 'void', with which Genesis begins. Blake believed in a dynamic and fiery primordial plenitude, an eternity in which unfallen, and uncreated, mankind was indistinguishable from God. Only when Urizen – the faculty of reason (to allegorize him a little simply) – withdraws or 'abstracts' from the eternal fluctuation and tries to quench it and contain it, do time and space begin, eternity roll away and chaos come. To create suns and moons and a globular earth is small compensation for the loss of eternity; indeed it only makes things worse. Once begun, nothing can stop the collapse until its hits bottom – that is, turns into the world as we know it, with shrunken human forms, as we know them, enslaved in Egypt. Blake continues his new Bible with *The Book of Ahania*, his Exodus, and then revisits some of the events of *Urizen* in *The Book of Los* (both 1795). Perhaps because he was now contemplating what we might call his 'epic of hell', however, he went no further with his Bible.

We have seen how frequently Blake evokes passages by his great predecessor John Milton. Like Wordsworth, Keats and Shelley, he believed that a poet's highest calling is to compose an epic in the Miltonic mode. Blake wrote three of them, and engraved and illuminated two. None of them is as long as *Paradise Lost*, but it appears from his letters that he once intended to write a single immense poem. The title-page of *Milton*, dated 1804, carries a subtitle, *a Poem in 12 Books*, altered to *2 Books* in some editions; the poem is certainly complete in only two books (fifty plates in one version), but an epic *about* Milton, Blake must have thought, requires twelve. On the title-page to *Jerusalem*, also dated 1804 but (like *Milton*) probably completed much later, Blake originally engraved 'in XXVIII Chapters' but deleted it before printing; the poem as we have it is in four chapters (ninety-nine plates). The third epic, first called *Vala* and then changed to *The Four Zoas*, survives only in manuscript on 133 pages, with eighty-four pages of drawings intended as illuminations, distributed over nine chapters or 'Nights'. Blake may have begun it as early as 1796 and continued working on it until about 1807, when he abandoned it for *Milton* and *Jerusalem*. (*Jerusalem* contains some passages from it virtually unaltered.) It shows several layers of revisions, including two versions of 'Night the Seventh', and there has been a good deal of debate over the order of pages and the sequence of corrections.

All three works, like *Paradise Lost,* deal with a vast range of events on many symbolic levels, from the Fall, seen from various angles, through biblical and European history, to an apocalypse of the poet's mission in these days and of the state of eternity he strives to bring about. Many of their great themes are extensions of those we found in the *Songs* and in *Thel*: fear of death and the construction of a Selfhood; fear of sexual love and the hypocrisies of repression; the deception of innocence by religion and the sacrifice or 'atonement' of innocence by priests and kings; the voluntary self-sacrifice of Jesus (and Milton) as a paradigm of the self-annihilation we are all called upon to undertake. Orc is here, too, but his role is diminished. In part, no doubt, because of the degeneration of the French Revolution into state tyranny and imperial conquest, the fiery Orc yields to the creative fires of Los the blacksmith, the figure of imagination and artistic creativity (and at times a stand-in for Blake himself): at one point Blake, Los, Milton and even Jesus seem to be merged into one man, whose task is to lead us to overcome tyranny and war through brotherhood and mutual forgiveness. This they are to do through precept and example, the precept being in the form of visions embodied in illuminated poetry, the example being that of Jesus, which we may all follow, through the death of our Selfhoods and the resurrection of our eternal selves.

Milton

I find *Milton* the most satisfying of the three. All of them contain difficult and abstract passages, catalogues of names and places, and an almost cavalier disregard of narrative conventions – one gets the impression that all the events in the epics occur simultaneously – but *Milton*, after a few dense opening pages, is organized fairly clearly around a fascinating central idea, the return of Milton from heaven. Wordsworth, as I mentioned in the last chapter, began a sonnet on the stagnant state of England in 1802 with the call, 'Milton! thou should'st be living at this hour.' Blake went one better than Wordsworth by bringing Milton back from the dead and setting him afoot in this dreary time. But he also went one better than Milton by getting him to purge himself of his errors – too much rational Calvinist theology, too much devotion to the classics ('the silly Greek & Latin slaves of the Sword', see Preface, line 10), his support of Cromwell, his divorce – and unite with William Blake, who, while free of those errors, desperately needed an ally of Milton's stature.

The poem begins, in fact, with a cry for help in the shape of a poem: 'Say first! what mov'd Milton ... To go into the deep ... What cause at length mov'd Milton to this unexampled deed? / A Bards prophetic Song!' (plate 2, lines 16–22). The song is an account of the Creation and Fall (a summary of *The Book of Urizen*), followed by an intricate dispute and its attempted settlement among several characters, three of whom are attributed with agricultural tools to complete specific tasks – to plough, to harrow and 'turn the Mills' (plate 4, line 10). The miller is Satan. Much of the story seems to reflect Blake's unhappiness during his three years at Felpham, where he felt stifled by the well-meant but trivial commissions that his patron William Hayley found for him to grind out; at least one quarrel must have arisen between them, mediated by several friends and by Catherine. Blake must have asked himself what Milton would have done, as 'The loud voic'd Bard terrify'd took refuge in Miltons bosom' (plate 14, line 9). Milton, in heaven, learns from this song that Satan, the principle of Selfhood, is still the lord of the world, and that it is partly his (Milton's) fault. *Paradise Lost* had punished Satan and his legions for disobedience by confining them to hell, or at least by banishing them from heaven. But from the Bard Milton hears that 'it is of Divine / Mercy alone! of Free Gift and Election that we live' (plate 13, lines 32–3) and not from vengeance, and he acknowledges that 'I in my Selfhood am that Satan'. So he descends to the land of the living – that is, 'Eternal Death' (plate 14, lines 30 and 32).

Most of Book I tells of the progress of Milton, or Milton's various aspects, through this world, and of his entry into Blake through his left foot, as if to join in Blake's pilgrimage of the spirit. Book II tells of a second descent, that of Ololon, Milton's female emanation, who also takes the burden of sin upon her and seeks to rejoin her alienated mate. Just what she represents it is difficult to say, but it may be relevant to remember Milton's praise of virginity (in *Comus* and elsewhere) and Oothoon's imaginative redefinition of it in Blake's *Visions*. Milton was separated from his wife, Mary, wrote a pamphlet urging the right of divorce and disinherited his daughters; it is, perhaps, Ololon's mission to set right these deeds by reuniting with Milton – sexually as well as spiritually (if there is any difference). At the climax of the poem Milton confronts Satan and announces that he will not annihilate him – for to do so is to become a Satan oneself – but will annihilate his own Selfhood, for

> Such are the Laws of Eternity that each shall mutually
> Annihilate himself for others good, as I for thee.

(plate 38, lines 35–6)

Satan will thus have nothing to do. At this point Albion, embodying the people of England, rises from his couch where he has been sleeping restlessly throughout the poem, takes a few steps and collapses back on to his couch. England is not yet ready, perhaps, but the means of rousing it are at hand. Then Milton faces Ololon, who has found him in Blake's garden, and gives a great speech that encapsulates most of Blake's most distinctive beliefs (plate 40, line 30, to plate 41, line 7).

> All that can be annihilated must be annihilated
> That the Children of Jerusalem may be saved from slavery
> There is a Negation, & there is a Contrary
> The Negation must be destroyd to redeem the Contraries
> The Negation is the Spectre; the Reasoning Power in Man
> This is a false Body: an Incrustation over my Immortal
> Spirit; a Selfhood, which must be put off & annihilated alway
> To cleanse the Face of my Spirit by Self-examination.
> To bathe in the Waters of Life; to wash off the Not Human
> I come in Self-annihilation & the grandeur of Inspiration
> To cast off Rational Demonstration by Faith in the Saviour
> To cast off the rotten rags of Memory by Inspiration
> To cast off Bacon, Locke & Newton from Albions covering
> To take off his filthy garments, & clothe him with Imagination
> To cast aside from Poetry, all that is not Inspiration[.]

Ololon then casts off her negative portion, Jesus appears in the midst of them, and Blake faints and revives to the vision of 'the Great Harvest & Vintage of the Nations' (plate 43) soon to be accomplished, as the agricultural work interrupted in the Bard's song is resumed by a newly inspiried poet-ploughman.

'Jerusalem'

The 'Preface' to *Milton* includes the famous stanzas sung under the name 'Jerusalem'.

> And did those feet in ancient time.
> Walk upon Englands mountains green:
> And was the holy Lamb of God,
> On Englands pleasant pastures seen!

During World War I the Poet Laureate Robert Bridges wrote to his friend the composer Hubert Parry with the suggestion that he set this poem to music. Parry did so, and the song was immediately adopted by the women's suffrage movement (it was sung at a Votes for Women concert at the Albert Hall in 1918) and then the labour movement. Workers sang it during the General Strike of 1926. The 'dark Satanic Mills' of the second stanza seemed a perfect phrase for the modern industrial factories of Britain, though Blake was probably not referring to factories when he wrote it. At the end of the strike, Prime Minister Stanley Baldwin made an appeal for reconciliation and forgiveness, and ended by quoting the final lines:

> I will not cease from Mental Fight,
> Nor shall my Sword sleep in my hand:
> Till we have built Jerusalem,
> In Englands green & pleasant Land.

Blake might have endorsed Baldwin's call for reconciliation, but he would have been chagrined to see his words 'adopted by both parties', as he said in another context. It is indeed sung today by the Left and the Right with equal fervour, and by millions of schoolchildren and churchgoers throughout the English-speaking world. (In American hymnals 'England' is generally replaced by 'Zion'.) The song has become 'religious', in Blake's special sense, as a cover for a false reconciliation between the generous and creative lambs and the greedy and oppressive wolves. If Blake returned from the dead like his hero Milton, he might hope that its words would burn some hypocritical lips. He might also hope that, if we sang it lustily enough, it might rouse us from our imaginative slumber so that we might take up the sword of mental fight.

Further Reading

Editions

All quotations of Blake's poetry in the present book have been taken from the Penguin Classics edition, *William Blake: The Complete Poems* (1977), edited by Alicia Ostriker and containing brief but useful notes. Any prose extracts are from David V. Erdman (ed.), *The Complete Poetry and Prose of William Blake*, 'newly revised edition' (1982 – available in paperback, Anchor Press), regarded as the standard edition of Blake. Like the Penguin edition, Erdman does not 'correct' or 'normalize' Blake's strange punctuation, and his conjectures as to punctuation and other blurry textual features are usually brilliant, though not universally accepted. He includes very few designs (the Penguin edition has none). In the back is a commentary by Harold Bloom on all the works but the *Songs*.

Students who want to make careful textual studies should also consult G. E. Bentley, jun. (ed.), *William Blake's Writings* (two volumes), in the Oxford English Texts series (1978). Bentley alters some punctuation (but indicates where he has done so) and includes a large portion of the designs in black and white.

Until Erdman's edition first appeared in 1965, the standard was that by Sir Geoffrey Keynes (*Complete Prose and Poetry of William Blake*), published in various formats and revisions from 1925 to 1974, and reissued by Reinhardt Books for The Nonesuch Press in 1989. Spelling is normalized here, and some editions have a few black-and-white designs.

There are two other editions that are very useful for the student, both in paperback. W. H. S. Stevenson's edition, *The Complete Poems*, in the Longman Annotated English Poets series (1971) contains all the poetry with copious and careful notes but no prose except *The Marriage* and no designs; spelling and punctuation are modernized. The Norton Critical Edition, *William Blake's Poetry and Designs*, by Mary Lynn Johnson and John E. Grant (1979), contains all the shorter works and *Milton* complete, together with a fair portion of the prose, but only excerpts from *The Four Zoas* and *Jerusalem*; original punctuation and layout are followed within reason. It has about eighty black-and-white designs and thirty-two plates in colour, as well as notes, maps and some critical essays.

118

The Oxford Authors edition, *Selected Works,* edited by Michael Mason (1988), contains all the poetry except *The Four Zoas* and *Ahania,* but in an eccentric arrangement by theme. The text is Bentley's modernized version.

There are many inexpensive smaller selections, nearly all of which will include the works discussed here, as will most large anthologies of Romantic poetry and many of eighteenth-century poetry.

Besides the Erdman edition or another full text, readers should make an effort to see facsimiles of the poetry as Blake originally produced it, in 'illuminated' form. Until recently there was *The Illuminated Blake,* edited by David V. Erdman (Anchor Press, 1974), which reproduced all the engraved poetry and *The Marriage* in black and white, with an often ingenious commentary, in an inexpensive paperback. Some enterprising publisher should bring it back. Still available, though more expensive, is David Bindman's *Complete Graphic Works of William Blake* (Putnam, 1978). Oxford University Press has issued (in paperback) two excellent colour facsimiles, the joint *Songs* (1970) and *The Marriage* (1975), with reading text and commentary by Sir Geoffrey Keynes. Dover has published separate colour facsimiles of *Innocence* (1971) and *Experience* (1984) as well as a joint volume of *America* and *Europe* (1983); they are not as good as the Oxford reproductions, but quite inexpensive.

The Trianon Press in Paris has produced extraordinarily true facsimiles of all the illuminated writings; they are also beyond the purse of ordinary mortals, so check the nearest research library to see if it has any of them. When in London, students should visit the permanent Blake exhibit at the Tate Gallery.

Biography

There is no really adequate biography of Blake, partly because not very many letters or reminiscences have come down to us. The standard is still Mona Wilson's *Life of William Blake* of 1927, edited by Geoffrey Keynes in 1971 (Oxford Univ. Press). The fullest source of information about Blake is G. E. Bentley, jun. (ed.), *Blake Records* (Oxford Univ. Press, 1969).

Criticism

Commentaries on Blake are legion and growing exponentially. The two greatest books (both Princeton Univ. Press) are Northrop Frye, *Fearful*

Symmetry: A Study of William Blake (1947) and David V. Erdman, *Blake: Prophet Against Empire* (1954; third edn, 1977). Neither is introductory, both are demanding, but eventually every student of Blake must read them.

Harold Bloom's commentary in the Erdman edition, and his *Blake's Apocalypse* (Cornell Univ. Press, 1963), are very interesting and helpful on all the poetry and some of the prose. He has strong views, and sounds far too confident of them, but his book is still the best general survey.

A good introduction to Blake's composite art (text and design together) is Jean H. Hagstrum, *William Blake: Poet and Painter* (Univ. of Chicago Press, 1964). A more advanced study is W. J. T. Mitchell, *Blake's Composite Art* (Princeton Univ. Press, 1978).

On the *Songs of Innocence and Experience,* see Robert F. Gleckner, *The Piper and the Bard* (Wayne State Univ. Press, 1959); Hazard Adams, *William Blake: A Reading of the Shorter Poems* (Univ. of Washington Press, 1963); E. D. Hirsch, *Innocence and Experience* (Yale Univ. Press, 1964); Zachary Leader, *Reading Blake's Songs* (Routledge & Kegan Paul, 1981); Heather Glen, *Vision and Disenchantment: Blake's Songs and Wordsworth's Lyrical Ballads* (Cambridge Univ. Press, 1983); Harold Pagliaro, *Selfhood and Redemption in Blake's Songs* (Pennsylvania State Univ. Press, 1987).

There are several useful anthologies of essays, such as Northrop Frye's volume on Blake in the 'Twentieth-Century Views' series (Prentice-Hall, 1966); Morton D. Paley's volume on the *Songs* in the 'Twentieth-Century Interpretations' series (Prentice-Hall, 1969); and Margaret Bottrall's volume on the *Songs* in the 'Casebook' series (Macmillan, 1969).

For a thorough and well-balanced survey of all Blake scholarship, see Mary Lynn Johnson's contribution to Frank Jordan (ed.), *The English Romantic Poets: A Review of Research and Criticism,* by the Modern Language Association (fourth edn, 1985).

Discover more about our forthcoming books through Penguin's FREE newspaper...

Penguin Quarterly

It's packed with:

- exciting features
- author interviews
- previews & reviews
- books from your favourite films & TV series
- exclusive competitions & much, much more...

Write off for your free copy today to:
Dept JC
Penguin Books Ltd
FREEPOST
West Drayton
Middlesex
UB7 0BR
NO STAMP REQUIRED

READ MORE IN PENGUIN

In every corner of the world, on every subject under the sun, Penguin represents quality and variety – the very best in publishing today.

For complete information about books available from Penguin – including Puffins, Penguin Classics and Arkana – and how to order them, write to us at the appropriate address below. Please note that for copyright reasons the selection of books varies from country to country.

In the United Kingdom: Please write to *Dept. JC, Penguin Books Ltd, FREEPOST, West Drayton, Middlesex UB7 OBR*.

If you have any difficulty in obtaining a title, please send your order with the correct money, plus ten per cent for postage and packaging, to *PO Box No. 11, West Drayton, Middlesex UB7 OBR*

In the United States: Please write to *Consumer Sales, Penguin USA, P.O. Box 999, Dept. 17109, Bergenfield, New Jersey 07621-0120*. VISA and MasterCard holders call 1-800-253-6476 to order all Penguin titles

In Canada: Please write to *Penguin Books Canada Ltd, 10 Alcorn Avenue, Suite 300, Toronto, Ontario M4V 3B2*

In Australia: Please write to *Penguin Books Australia Ltd, P.O. Box 257, Ringwood, Victoria 3134*

In New Zealand: Please write to *Penguin Books (NZ) Ltd, Private Bag 102902, North Shore Mail Centre, Auckland 10*

In India: Please write to *Penguin Books India Pvt Ltd, 706 Eros Apartments, 56 Nehru Place, New Delhi 110 019*

In the Netherlands: Please write to *Penguin Books Netherlands bv, Postbus 3507, NL-1001 AH Amsterdam*

In Germany: Please write to *Penguin Books Deutschland GmbH, Metzlerstrasse 26, 60594 Frankfurt am Main*

In Spain: Please write to *Penguin Books S. A., Bravo Murillo 19, 1° B, 28015 Madrid*

In Italy: Please write to *Penguin Italia s.r.l., Via Felice Casati 20, I–20124 Milano*

In France: Please write to *Penguin France S. A., 17 rue Lejeune, F–31000 Toulouse*

In Japan: Please write to *Penguin Books Japan, Ishikiribashi Building, 2–5–4, Suido, Bunkyo-ku, Tokyo 112*

In Greece: Please write to *Penguin Hellas Ltd, Dimocritou 3, GR–106 71 Athens*

In South Africa: Please write to *Longman Penguin Southern Africa (Pty) Ltd, Private Bag X08, Bertsham 2013*

PENGUIN AUDIOBOOKS

A Quality of Writing that Speaks for Itself

Penguin Books has always led the field in quality publishing. Now you can listen at leisure to your favourite books, read to you by familiar voices from radio, stage and screen. Penguin Audiobooks are ideal as gifts, for when you are travelling or simply to enjoy at home. They are produced to an excellent standard, and abridgements are always faithful to the original texts. From thrillers to classic literature, biography to humour, with a wealth of titles in between, Penguin Audiobooks offer you quality, entertainment and the chance to rediscover the pleasure of listening.

You can order Penguin Audiobooks through Penguin Direct by telephoning (0181) 899 4036. The lines are open 24 hours every day. Ask for Penguin Direct, quoting your credit card details.

Published or forthcoming:

Emma by Jane Austen, read by Fiona Shaw

Persuasion by Jane Austen, read by Joanna David

Pride and Prejudice by Jane Austen, read by Geraldine McEwan

The Tenant of Wildfell Hall by Anne Brontë, read by Juliet Stevenson

Jane Eyre by Charlotte Brontë, read by Juliet Stevenson

Villette by Charlotte Brontë, read by Juliet Stevenson

Wuthering Heights by Emily Brontë, read by Juliet Stevenson

The Woman in White by Wilkie Collins, read by Nigel Anthony and Susan Jameson

Heart of Darkness by Joseph Conrad, read by David Threlfall

Tales from the One Thousand and One Nights, read by Souad Faress and Raad Rawi

Moll Flanders by Daniel Defoe, read by Frances Barber

Great Expectations by Charles Dickens, read by Hugh Laurie

Hard Times by Charles Dickens, read by Michael Pennington

Martin Chuzzlewit by Charles Dickens, read by John Wells

The Old Curiosity Shop by Charles Dickens, read by Alec McCowen

PENGUIN AUDIOBOOKS

Crime and Punishment by Fyodor Dostoyevsky, read by Alex Jennings
Middlemarch by George Eliot, read by Harriet Walter
Silas Marner by George Eliot, read by Tim Pigott-Smith
The Great Gatsby by F. Scott Fitzgerald, read by Marcus D'Amico
Madame Bovary by Gustave Flaubert, read by Claire Bloom
Jude the Obscure by Thomas Hardy, read by Samuel West
The Return of the Native by Thomas Hardy, read by Steven Pacey
Tess of the D'Urbervilles by Thomas Hardy, read by Eleanor Bron
The Iliad by Homer, read by Derek Jacobi
Dubliners by James Joyce, read by Gerard McSorley
The Dead and Other Stories by James Joyce, read by Gerard McSorley
On the Road by Jack Kerouac, read by David Carradine
Sons and Lovers by D. H. Lawrence, read by Paul Copley
The Fall of the House of Usher by Edgar Allan Poe, read by Andrew Sachs
Wide Sargasso Sea by Jean Rhys, read by Jane Lapotaire and Michael Kitchen
The Little Prince by Antoine de Saint-Exupéry, read by Michael Maloney
Frankenstein by Mary Shelley, read by Richard Pasco
Of Mice and Men by John Steinbeck, read by Gary Sinise
Travels with Charley by John Steinbeck, read by Gary Sinise
The Pearl by John Steinbeck, read by Hector Elizondo
Dr Jekyll and Mr Hyde by Robert Louis Stevenson, read by Jonathan Hyde
Kidnapped by Robert Louis Stevenson, read by Robbie Coltrane
The Age of Innocence by Edith Wharton, read by Kerry Shale
The Buccaneers by Edith Wharton, read by Dana Ivey
Mrs Dalloway by Virginia Woolf, read by Eileen Atkins

READ MORE IN PENGUIN

CRITICAL STUDIES

Described by *The Times Educational Supplement* as 'admirable' and 'superb', Penguin Critical Studies is a specially developed series of critical essays on the major works of literature for use by students in universities, colleges and schools.

Titles published or in preparation include:

READ MORE IN PENGUIN

CRITICAL STUDIES

Described by *The Times Educational Supplement* as 'admirable' and 'superb', Penguin Critical Studies is a specially developed series of critical essays on the major works of literature for use by students in universities, colleges and schools.

Titles published or in preparation include:

SHAKESPEARE

Antony and Cleopatra
As You Like It
Coriolanus
Henry IV Part 2
Hamlet
Julius Caesar
King Lear
The Merchant of Venice
A Midsummer Night's Dream
Much Ado About Nothing
Othello
Richard II
Richard III
Romeo and Juliet
Shakespeare – Text into Performance
Shakespeare's History Plays
The Tempest
Troilus and Cressida
Twelfth Night
The Winter's Tale

CHAUCER

Chaucer
The Pardoner's Tale
**The Prologue to The
  Canterbury Tales**

READ MORE IN PENGUIN

POETRY LIBRARY

Arnold	Selected by Kenneth Allott
Blake	Selected by W. H. Stevenson
Browning	Selected by Daniel Karlin
Burns	Selected by Angus Calder and William Donnelly
Byron	Selected by A. S. B. Glover
Clare	Selected by Geoffrey Summerfield
Coleridge	Selected by Richard Holmes
Donne	Selected by John Hayward
Dryden	Selected by Douglas Grant
Hardy	Selected by David Wright
Herbert	Selected by W. H. Auden
Jonson	Selected by George Parfitt
Keats	Selected by John Barnard
Kipling	Selected by James Cochrane
Lawrence	Selected by Keith Sagar
Milton	Selected by Laurence D. Lerner
Pope	Selected by Douglas Grant
Rubáiyát of Omar Khayyám	Translated by Edward FitzGerald
Shelley	Selected by Isabel Quigley
Tennyson	Selected by W. E. Williams
Wordsworth	Selected by Nicholas Roe
Yeats	Selected by Timothy Webb